What People Are Saying about Mani Erfan and *True Wealth*...

"Mani Erfan's book *True Wealth* is a rare gem! It is full of riveting, inspiring, and encouraging testimonies, case studies, and wise counsel from end to end. Like a great business or entrepreneur, it under-promises and over-delivers. It's just the shot in the arm or kick in the butt that many of us need to let go of our excuses, get out of our comfort zones, and pursue our God-given dreams and destinies. It's the best book I have read in a long time. Buy it. Read it. Do it."

—*Dr. Bruce Cook*
Chairman and CEO, VentureAdvisers, Inc.
Kingdom House Publishing
Kingdom Congressional International Alliance
Seattle, WA

"Intriguing and inspiring! In fact, I found myself thinking, *This book would be a great storyline for a movie*. It is filled with many compelling true-life stories. There are great analogies, as well as motivating and thought-provoking themes. This book is not written from the high tower of theoretical ideas, but from the real-life experiences of a man who's proven that there are no challenges or obstacles in life that cannot be overcome by the abounding grace of God. Mani is uniquely gifted in both business and ministry. His passion for the Lord fills him with a compassion for people that drives him with an unparalleled energy. As you read *True Wealth,* I am certain you will find yourself deeply encouraged and motivated in your own life. You, too, can become a catalyst for success!"

—*Doug Stringer*
Founder, Somebody Cares America/International
Turning Point Ministries International
Author, *Leadership Awakening* and *In Search of a Father's Blessing*

"Have you had difficult challenges? How about escape from Iran, near false imprisonment, numerous business missteps, battling giants! Mani offers a no-fluff practical guide with clear and proven strategic business guidelines to transform your "impossible" into *True Wealth*. Nothing to millions—it can happen for you. This is a must-read as we enter God's wealth transfer season."

—*Dr. Erik A. Kudlis*
CEO, Erik's Design Build Associates, Inc.

"Mani Erfan's *True Wealth* provides compelling and invaluable insights on the challenges, risks, and rewards of following Christ in business and in life. Captivating, encouraging, and inspiring—this book is a message of hope, encouragement, and redemption."

—*Douglas F. Wall*
Author, *Redemption: God's Power to Reach the Least, the Last and the Lost*
Managing Director, Life Ventures
Cofounder, PureForge
San Diego, CA

"Mani's escape from Iran, engineered by his daring father, is breathtaking. That by itself is an interest magnet to read this book. But there is more, much more! Once a Muslim and now a powerful man of God, Mani is boldly raising up a new generation of Christian pioneers in Iran and in other suppressed eastern and Middle Eastern countries. He has no fear and walks the talk that, with God, all things are possible. Mani is immensely successful in business, richly anointed by the Holy Spirit, and firmly confident in his identity. This book will stimulate you and stir your Spirit to soar where you have not gone before!"

—*Frank Amedia*
Pastor, Touch Heaven Ministries
Canfield, OH

TRUE WEALTH

TRUE WEALTH

HOW TO FULFILL YOUR DREAMS WITHOUT LOSING YOUR SOUL

MANI ERFAN

WHITAKER HOUSE

True Wealth:
How to Fulfill Your Dreams Without Losing Your Soul

manierfan.com

ISBN: 978-1-62911-988-5
eBook ISBN: 978-1-62911-989-2
Printed in the United States of America

Whitaker House
1030 Hunt Valley Circle
New Kensington, PA 15068
www.whitakerhouse.com

Library of Congress Cataloging-in-Publication Data (Pending)

1 2 3 4 5 6 7 8 9 10 11 25 24 23 22 21 20 19 18

CONTENTS

PART 1:
THE UNICAT STORY

1

EVERY STORY HAS A BEGINNING

I have always dreamed of owning my own business. The idea took root in my heart before I reached my teenage years. I was born in a modern household in Tehran, Iran, when the country was still ruled by the Shah Mohammad Reva Pahlavi, the last shah in Iran's monarchy. Under the shah, the country was far more westernized than it is today. We had Western clothes, hairstyles, and modern music.

My father, Iraj Erfan, was born in the Soviet Union but immigrated to Iran with his family at a very young age. He became a professional soccer player and an Olympian star, playing on Iran's national soccer team. After my father retired from athletics, he joined the newly created Iranian Airlines and became a very successful and sought-after pilot. My mother, Behjat Shakibi, an Iranian, was born to Kurdish parents in northern Iran. Her father was a highly educated man who taught himself to speak French and Arabic in the early 1920s, when most people in Iran couldn't read or write.

My childhood was an exciting adventure. As a pilot, my father was awarded free airline tickets for his family to travel the world. I visited the United States, the United Kingdom, China, Japan, and Italy before I turned twelve years old. My parents considered themselves Muslim, but my religious upbringing was negligible. My only spiritual influence was my devout Muslim grandmother, who took care of me when my parents traveled together. I clearly remember her praying the Muslim prayer five times a day every time I stayed with her.

My hardworking parents expected excellence from me, and I worked hard to deliver. By the time I became a teenager, I spoke fluent English, played classical piano, and trained daily to qualify for the Iranian youth tennis team. I was never a rebellious child, and although I had no serious religious training, I was taught to be a moral person, knowing right from wrong. My life goal was to be successful and to do everything I could to make my parents proud.

The Islamic Revolution

Life in Iran changed dramatically in early 1979. After a thirty-year reign, Shah Pahlavi and his family fled the country. Pahlavi was Iran's last shah of the 2,500-year monarchial rule, dating back to the founding of the Persian Empire. It was a cataclysmic change for the Iranian people. Some of us were affected more than others.

At the time the shah fled, the Islamic spiritual leader, Sayyid Ruhollah Mūsavi Khomeini, returned from exile in Europe to bring fundamental Islam and Sharia law to Iran. On April 1, 1979, Iran was officially declared an Islamic Republic.

The advent of the Islamic revolution changed everything in my life. My world was turned upside down. At thirteen years old, I went from a free lifestyle with little religious influence to being smothered by the Islamic faith and culture and required to follow all its teachings, whether I liked them or not. We were immersed in religious fervor and baptized in stringent Islamic rules that affected every aspect of our lives. How we dressed, what we ate, what music we could listen to, what movies we could watch, which people we could associate with—every detail of our lives was under a microscope.

For the first time in my life, rebellion flared up within me. I didn't want to blindly follow all the Islamic beliefs and regulations. I protested every step of the way. If the government wanted me to cut my hair short, I wanted to keep it long. If they forbade me to wear short pants, I would put them on and walk out the door. When all styles of music were banned by Ayatollah Khomeini for a short time in the early 1980s, I played my piano even louder. I was running headlong toward trouble, and, if I wasn't careful, I would find myself locked in a prison cell somewhere deep in Iran.

I didn't want to blindly follow all the Islamic beliefs and regulations. I protested every step of the way.... I was running headlong toward trouble, and, if I wasn't careful, I would find myself locked in a prison cell somewhere deep in Iran.

The most painful part of the revolution was watching my lifelong dream of studying in the United States evaporate before my eyes. In 1979, a group of radical Islamic students overran the US embassy in Tehran and held fifty-two American citizens hostage for four hundred forty-four days. Political relations between Iran and the United States, once friendly, were now shattered.

Desperate to Escape

Things came to a head for me in 1983. Although the US hostages had been released two years earlier, Iran was in the middle of a war with Saddam Hussein and Iraq—a war it is still ill-prepared to fight. By then, I was sixteen years old, a junior in high school, and desperately looking for a way to escape Iran and my mandatory conscription into the Iranian Army.

Under the ayatollah, every able-bodied eighteen-year-old male was required to serve two years in the military. The war was raging on, and Saddam Hussein, in defiance of international law, was using chemical weapons on the front lines. The Iranian army was scrambling for a strategy to win the war. Desperate to push the Iraqi army out of occupied territories, Iran used human wave attacks, just throwing young fighters by the thousands into battle. This led to massive and devastating casualties.

Young men that I had known since early childhood were sent to the front lines and never came back, or they returned severely maimed by chemical burns and other horrors of war. Many of them, filled with tremendous zeal for the Islamic Revolution and its fanatic leader Khomeini, went willingly to battle. However, casualties were high—about ten to fifteen thousand Iranian soldiers died per engagement, and there was always a shortage of able-bodied men. My prospects of surviving a two-year stint in the Iranian armed forces were grim.

My choices in life were frightening: either be drafted and die in the war or be thrown into a prison cell, ending up standing in front of a firing squad for constantly acting out against the revolution.

But there was a dangerous third option. I could leave Iran immediately. My parents were convinced that they could no longer protect me, but how would I escape? All young Iranian men, sixteen years and older, were forbidden to leave the country until they had military discharge papers, and that was clearly not an option for me!

A Father's Unconditional Love

Daily, I begged my parents to find a way for me to escape. The most commonly used scheme for fleeing Iran was taking an overland route to Turkey aided by smugglers. This choice was extremely dangerous, as the smugglers traveled through treacherous mountain passages and were often caught by the Iranian border police. Any form of military engagement had deadly consequences for both the smuggler and the one being smuggled. To make matters worse, even if I made it across the border, I would be a nation-less refugee in a foreign land without a legal passport. I would be forced to remain in Turkey for years and likely fail to gain permission to immigrate to my ultimate destination—the United States of America.

Was there another option? The dangers I faced were frightfully real. Each day, feelings of hopelessness grew.

I can still clearly remember my parents' nightly arguments about the best way to help me. Then, in the middle of the conflict, my father devised a radical plan for my escape. His actions on my behalf the summer of 1983 were incredible feats of courage and self-sacrifice, the full expression of a father's love for his only son, without any concern for his own well-being.

During his years flying for Iran Air, my father had gained recognition as one of the most skilled pilots in the country, which made him a valuable asset to the Iranian government and the captain who was always chosen to fly influential government leaders to international conferences. It was during one of those sensitive flights in June 1983, when my father flew the speaker of the Iranian Parliament and other statesmen to a neighboring Arab country, that he made his courageous move.

Sitting on the runway of the Mehrabad International Airport in Tehran, the aircraft was positioned for takeoff, with an armed military guard in the cockpit and the who's who of Iranian political leadership in the cabin. Without warning, my father taxied the plane to the left. He blocked the runway, refusing to take off and demanding to speak to the most important passenger onboard, speaker of the Parliament, Ayatollah Akbar Hashemi Rafsanjani.

Without warning, my father taxied the plane to the left. He blocked the runway, refusing to take off and demanding to speak to the most important passenger onboard, speaker of the Parliament, Ayatollah Akbar Hashemi Rafsanjani.

Pandemonium erupted in the cockpit. The armed guard thrust his gun into the back of my father's head, demanding that he take off immediately. Without flinching, my father shouted back, "I will not fly until I speak to Ayatollah Rafsanjani." He turned to his copilot, who sat paralyzed with fear, and forbade him to take any action as long as he remained the captain.

Within moments, the news reached the passengers, and there was panic as they braced for a terrorist attack. Military guards raced to the cockpit and surrounded my father with guns cocked. Still he demanded to speak to Ayatollah Rafsanjani.

In spite of protests for his safety, Ayatollah Rafsanjani walked into the cockpit to personally talk to my father. After calming the guards, Rafsanjani was short and to the point.

"I understand that you wish to see me, Captain?" Rafsanjani said with steely precision. "What can I do for you?"

"Mr. Rafsanjani, I am sorry that I had to get your attention this way," my father replied respectfully, "but I have been trying to reach you at your office for months without success, and this is my only chance to speak with you."

"Tell me, Captain, what is so important that you would recklessly cause all of this commotion and make many of our friends nervous for their lives?"

"Mr. Rafsanjani, I have a son, and he is my only son. He is bright, very intelligent, and has dreamed of studying abroad. I know that many young men are risking their lives fighting for our country, but I am asking for your permission for my son to legally leave Iran to pursue his studies. You never know, sir; if you save his life today, one day he may save the lives of many of his countrymen."

"Is this all you need, Captain? Was all of this about your son?"

"Yes, sir. May I have your word that you will allow him to leave? I am serving my country, and I will continue to do so as long as I am needed."

"Yes, Captain Erfan," Rafsanjani's replied. "Upon our return, please come to my office, and I will have the paperwork for you to get your son's passport. I will even grant him a government scholarship to help defray the cost of his studies. Now, can we get this plane off the ground? Our friends are waiting for us."

My father should have been arrested on the spot, dragged off to Evin Prison, Iran's most notorious prison, and never heard from again. Fortunately, that did not happen. In moments, the crisis was averted. In today's world of terrorism, it is hard to believe that after my father's demands, the Iranian leaders still entrusted him with their safety in the air! He flew them without further incident to their destination and home again.

There was great celebration in the Erfan home upon my father's return the next day. I had permission to legally leave the country! I would not have to face the treacherous mountain paths to Turkey or the Iraqi soldiers in war. I could pursue my education and my dreams. One week later, separated from my family, I watched Iran disappear slowly from sight as I headed to my new destiny. My father's sacrifice ultimately cost him his job and, for a short time, his freedom, but it gave me life and the chance to live out my destiny and my calling.

The sacrifice of a father became life to his son.

2

THE GREAT ESCAPE

I could hardly believe I was free! Just a few days after I landed in Bonn, Germany, I turned seventeen, the age in which it would have been impossible to leave Iran, even with a letter from Ayatollah Rafsanjani. Boy, did I feel lucky. Yet, even though I was no longer in Iran, my final destination was the United States, and no one was handing out invitations to Iranian seventeen-year-olds to study there. Three times I tried to get a US visa, without success; I received a rejection stamp on my passport each time.

Discouraged, exhausted, and afraid, I knew in my heart that I did not belong in Europe. I had longed to live in the United States for as long as I could remember. But by the time I received a third rejection stamp from the US embassy in Bonn, I was sure that my chances to make it to the States were slim to none. No one with three rejection stamps had ever gotten a visa before. Reluctantly, I began to plan for studies in Germany. My parents joined me in Bonn to help me decide what to do next. As they researched the right school for me to attend in Germany, I silently repeated, *This isn't right. This isn't right.*

I wanted one last chance to fulfill my dream.

"Let's travel to another country and try one more US embassy," I begged my parents. "One more try. Please, if it doesn't work, I will stay right here in Europe."

My father never stopped believing in me, so he agreed that we would take one last shot. We had nothing to lose. We booked a flight, and the three of us flew to London.

An Unexpected Friend

The best chance we had of succeeding was for my father to go to the large US embassy in London to plead my case. When he returned to our hotel room with an account of his first day at the embassy, it threw our family into turmoil once again.

While standing in a long line for my visa, my father heard a voice from his past.

"Iraj Erfan! What are you doing waiting in a queue at the US embassy, my friend?"

Startled, my father looked up to see an old friend who had left Iran a few years earlier. After they exchanged greetings, my father explained my impossible situation, the three rejection stamps from Germany, and our one last hope.

"Do not worry, Iraj," the man said encouragingly. "Let me have your son's passport and his visa documents, and leave it in my hands. I will have a visa for you by tomorrow."

Without asking a single question, or having any idea what position this man held with the government that gave him such influence, my father excitedly handed over all my papers, plus a thousand pounds sterling for his friend's trouble. He walked back to our hotel with a light step, certain that all our problems would be resolved the next day.

My mother was furious! "What do you mean you just gave Mani's passport and money to this man? Are you crazy? Out of your mind? You didn't ask where he lived, where he worked, for his phone number! How do you know that we will ever hear from him again? How can Mani go to school or even get into another country without his passport? Now, we can't even go back to Germany!"

Realizing how naive he had been, my father stood there in shock. It had never occurred to him to doubt his friend's honesty. Realizing he may have made a serious mistake, he spent a long, stressful night pacing the hotel room floor. I spent the night tossing and turning in that unfamiliar hotel bed, fearing the worst. The next morning, bleary-eyed from a restless night, my father went downstairs to the hotel lobby to wait. Would my visa ever arrive? (Those were the days before cell phones, when there was no easy way to remain in constant communication with someone. Then, of course, my father didn't even have a telephone number to reach his friend!) The hours of waiting were unbearable.

Fortunately, my father's trusting nature was rewarded! The gentleman showed up that afternoon, not only with my passport, but also with a visa for entry into the United States stamped inside, just as he had promised. Another obstacle had been overcome on my behalf!

No words could express the joy we experienced inside our little hotel room near Heathrow Airport. I should have never received that visa after three prior rejections, but there it was, right smack in the middle of my passport. I was astounded by my good fortune. Could all of this really be a coincidence? Strangely enough, after that chance meeting, my father never saw or heard from his friend again.

Two days later, I was walking through Heathrow Airport with my suitcase in one hand and a one-way ticket to Philadelphia in the other. I remember standing beside my father on the elevator as we made our way to the boarding gate. I knew that my life was about to change forever. At seventeen years old, I was going to be separated from the people who truly loved me and begin life on my own. I was shaking with both fear and excitement. I grabbed my father's hand and shook it, and, as I looked at his tear-filled eyes, my own eyes filled with tears.

I knew that my life was about to change forever. At seventeen years old, I was going to be separated from the people who truly loved me and begin life on my own. I was shaking with both fear and excitement.

"I promise you, Dad, I will succeed in America. I will make you proud! You will never regret your sacrifices in sending me. I promise you, Dad, I will succeed!"

With those words, I walked through the airport gate and into my new life.

How Life Can Collapse in a Split Second

Now let's fast forward four years later to May 1987. I was a twenty-year-old chemical engineering student at the University of Florida in Gainesville. Life was good and all under control, or so I thought. I was an excellent student, with a good paying engineering internship and a serious relationship with my college sweetheart, and my future seemed secure. I was fulfilling the promise to my dad—my success would make him so proud.

Then, in just a few short days, my entire life collapsed around me. It all started with breaking up with my girlfriend or, should I say, her breaking up with me. I was heartbroken, because I believed we were in love for life. When I heard that she had feelings for another man, I just exploded. In a very heated moment, hurling hurtful words in haste and anger, I told her that one day I would get even with her.

In response, she felt the need to go to the authorities and accuse me of things I had never done. Her accusations and hysterical tears set off a horrific chain of events. I was falsely accused of a crime, arrested by the police, and put in jail. As soon as word got out, I was suspended from school, fired from my internship, and all my friendships suddenly disappeared.

My money was gone, as well, since I had spent most of my savings on lawyers. Now, without a job, I had no means of replenishing it. I lost my sense of peace, direction, value, and purpose. I lived in a constant state of fear and loss. I was too proud to contact my parents, who were still living in Iran, to tell them what was happening and that I needed them. I was facing the collapse of my life all on my own.

I had never been religious person, and I was definitely not a practicing Muslim at the time. However, I was suddenly convinced that my desperate situation required some form of heavenly intervention, so I started to seek Allah for help. It was an unusual decision for me. I had not called on the "Big Guy" for a long time, and I wasn't sure if he was going to respond. In the Islam faith, if you don't do what you are supposed to do for Allah, he is not obligated to do anything for you in return. It is a give-and-take relationship, without any grace, and I had not been giving much from my end since I was a little boy.

As the weeks passed, all my cries and pleas to Allah went unheard, and I was getting closer and closer to the court date, when my fate would be decided. If the judge believed the false accusations about me, I would face a possible twenty-year jail sentence. The pain and anxiety of my uncertain future, the loneliness of my life, and the financial ruin took a serious toll on me. I would wake up two or three times every night in a cold sweat. I couldn't eat. I was tortured with the picture of my parents' faces when they heard the news. If I was convicted and ended up in prison, how would I ever face my father, who had risked everything for me? Thoughts of suicide crossed my mind all the time. I finally decided that, if convicted, I would end it all rather than face a lifetime of humiliation.

One Person's Compassion Rescued Me

Three months earlier, on the day I was arrested, I sat in a jail cell in a state of despair. Out of all my Iranian and American friends, only one person came to visit me. His name was Jeff, a fellow chemical engineering student who was several years older. Jeff had been in the military for a while, and the government was paying for him to get a degree. He had befriended me before all this trouble began, and I knew from our conversations that he was a good family man with a sincere Christian faith.

I wish I could forget that painful day as I sat behind a glass wall that separated us. I wanted to say something to Jeff, to protest my innocence, to tell him how frightened I felt, but I couldn't put the words together. Succumbing to my fear and grief, I sat and cried like a baby. When I looked up, I noticed that tears were flowing down Jeff's face, and with no words spoken, we sat there for a long time.

After Jeff left, I walked back to my cell and thought to myself, *Jeff is a good Christian man, and he must really care about me.* I could not recall meeting a man of faith who acted with that kind of compassion ever before.

Jeff didn't disappear after that, either. Over the next three months as I awaited my trial, he spent time with me, asked me to have coffee with him, invited me to his home, and checked in to make sure I was doing okay. As my court date approached, Jeff invited me to a weekend business conference in Tampa, Florida. It was July, the court date was just ten days away, and my stress levels had become unbearable. The business conference was going to cost me one hundred fifty dollars, and I had less than two hundred dollars in my bank account. It didn't make a bit of sense to spend most of it on a business function when there was a chance I would be in a prison cell in a few weeks. But, inexplicably, I registered for the event, not realizing that what would happen in Tampa would be life-altering.

The first two days of the conference were aggravating. I was so distraught about my situation that I couldn't focus. I wasn't getting a thing out of the panels or business discussions. "Why am I here?" I muttered. At the end of the Saturday night session, the speaker announced that there would be one last meeting the following morning.

As soon as I entered the meeting room Sunday morning, I knew it was not a typical business gathering. Worship music, people praying—whoa, wait a minute! I didn't sign up for this. No one told me this last meeting was going to be a church service. How had I missed this? I wanted to bolt to the door! But the idea of showing such disrespect for Jeff after he had been so good to me kept me in my seat. I cannot tell you what the message was about or even if I enjoyed it. In fact, all I can recall is that I wanted to sneak out without making a scene.

At the end of the service, the speaker asked everyone to stand up. We were all standing around the conference tables when he invited people who wanted prayer or to give their lives to Christ to come up front. That was certainly not *my* plan.

Then, out of nowhere, I felt a push from behind. It was forceful enough that I had to grab the chair in front of me so that I would not fall. *Who did that?* I wondered silently in frustration. *Don't you Christians have any courtesy? If I want to go, I will go myself. You don't have to push me!*

The speaker made a second call for prayer, and again I felt a hard push from behind. This time, I spun around to see who was playing tricks. No one was there! Everyone was standing, heads down, praying, and there was no sign of a potential culprit anywhere. *I must be losing my mind! All the stress of the last several months—now I'm imagining things.*

The Christian speaker continued to encourage us in prayer—wham!—my knees buckled, and I fell to the ground, still holding onto the chair in front of me for dear life. Although no one was there, I could feel hands and knees pressing me from behind, urging me to go forward, as I resisted with every bit of my willpower. *I am not even a practicing Muslim,* I thought. *This stubborn and prideful Iranian Muslim boy is not going forward!*

Finally, it was over. I felt the release of the pressure on my back, and as I stood up, my first thought was *escape!* I quickly grabbed my stuff from the table, intent on finding the nearest exit door and running for my life!

Just as I was about to leave, one of Jeff's friends stopped me to ask how I liked the morning service. I had every intention of making some milquetoast comment that it was nice, thank you so much, blah, blah, blah. But what came out of my mouth shocked both of us: "I believe in the Lord Jesus Christ as my Lord and Savior." *What? What did I just blurt out? Did I just say what I think I said? Where did those words come from?*

I had every intention of making some milquetoast comment that it was nice, thank you so much, blah, blah, blah. But what came out of my mouth shocked both of us: "I believe in the Lord Jesus Christ as my Lord and Savior."

Seeming surprised but pleased, he said, "Mani, wait a minute. Let me go get Jeff."

I thought, *Yes, you go get Jeff. I'm going to run out of here as fast as I can and go where no one can find me!* I walked speedily toward the door when another man greeted me and asked how I was doing. My response to him was the same: "I believe in the Lord Jesus Christ as my Lord and Savior." *What? Again? What is happening to me?* As I turned away, I bumped into the preacher, and you can guess how that conversation went!

I had confessed Jesus is Lord to three people within 10 minutes, and I was in great confusion. *Am I not a Muslim? Don't I have enough problems of my own, without adding this to the long list? Haven't I been taught that if one leaves the Islam faith, he is a* kaferim *and condemned to hell? Do I really need to add hell to my list of problems?* But then I recalled that I had called on the name of Allah for months, and nothing had happened. I was getting desperate, and this very strange thing was taking place. Maybe, just maybe, this Jesus Christ could help me.

Finally, I reached my hotel room. All alone, I knelt for the first time in my life to pray. I asked this Christian God to show me if He was real, if He really existed. I poured out all my problems and my heartache before Him, not realizing that He already knew it all. Then, I offered what I thought was the deal of the century: "God, if you fix all my problems within seven days, before my court date, I will serve you for the rest of my life. And if you don't, then I will know you don't exist. Oh, by the way, I ask this in the name of Jesus, who I professed three times to be my Lord and who Christians claim to be the Son of God."

Although I never recommend making deals with God as a way of salvation, this is what happened between Him and me. I guess He knew my heart and could tell that I was serious in proposing this exchange. Now here I am, thirty years later, still serving Him with all my heart.

Seven Amazing Days

From the moment I stood up from that prayer, miracles started happening. The first miracle was peace. I felt an immediate sense of comfort and rest. I believed that everything was going to be okay, and I started to sing—funny, since I didn't know any hymns or worship songs. I began to sing rock-and-roll songs by Def Leppard (you would know them if you lived through the eighties) driving all the way back to Gainesville. I slept like a baby that night, without waking up until morning.

The next day, when I went to the bank to withdraw the last fifteen dollars from my account, I received the first financial miracle of my life. I asked the teller to close my account and give me the money that was left.

She responded, "Do you want all the money in your account, sir?"

Well, that's strange, I thought, *since I only have fifteen dollars in there.*

"Yes, I want all of it, of course!"

"Okay, all two thousand and fifteen dollars. Do you want it in large or small bills?"

"What? Did I hear you right? I have two thousand and fifteen dollars? Are you sure you have the right account?"

"Yes, sir, it is the right account."

I finally resigned to the money being in my account. I was certain it was a bank error, and I dared not touch it, so I cancelled the withdrawal. However, there were no errors, and the money remained in my account. I know that God used some human agent to bless me that day, but I saw God's hand all over it. To this day, I don't know who put that money in my bank account.

On Thursday of that same week, four days after I prayed to God to reveal Himself to me, I received a call from my attorney. I had hired him months earlier, paid him most of my savings, and not heard from him since. In fact, I had concluded that the man was not interested in the case at all and that I would face all my legal troubles on my own.

His call was my third miracle of the week. My case had been dropped by the state of Florida, and all charges against me were removed from the record! I could hardly believe my ears! The court recognized that there was no proof for the false accusations brought against me. I was free and clear of all charges, and I could immediately return to school and to my internship if I wished. I was beyond elated! In a matter of four days, I had received almost everything I had asked from God.

The last miracle came on Friday, when I unexpectedly saw my ex-girlfriend standing along the street waiting for a ride. Because our breakup had led me to a downward spiral, I had been angry with her for a while, but I had asked God for the miracle of forgiveness and the strength to let it go. Seeing her standing on the side of the street, I was certain that it was another answer to my prayers.

I pulled up next to her and called out, "Are you looking for a ride?"

Cautiously, she answered yes, seeming unsure if she should get into the car with me.

As I drove her to her destination, an amazing sense of grace and forgiveness came over me. I looked at her and said, "You know, no matter what happened between us, I still love you. I am willing to let the past go and forgive you, if you can also forgive me. We can start from where we left off months back."

After her initial shock, she asked, "Are you really able to forgive this whole mess? You know I never intended to hurt you like this."

"I know," I answered quietly, "and I forgive you. What do you want to do now?"

"I love him, Mani," she responded quietly, referring to the other guy. "I want you to let me go."

Her response would have crushed me just a few days earlier, but when she asked me to let her go, I felt peace. Instead of the piercing pain of rejection, I experienced a deep sense of release. I realized that God had accepted me, and I did not need the acceptance of another person to make me whole. I gracefully told her that I released her, and I wished the very best for her.

> *Everything I had asked God for had come to pass in just five days, and now I was certain that He was real. It was my turn to fulfill my part of the bargain.*

As I drove off, all I could think about was the final miracle I had just experienced. Everything I had asked God for had come to pass in just five days, and now I was certain that He was real. It was my turn to fulfill my part of the bargain.

The Greatest Thing of All

Once I got home, I picked up the phone and called Jeff, excited to share the miracle that had just occurred. Then I asked him for two things: a Bible and a list of all the rules and regulations I would need to follow to be a good Christian. As a former Muslim, I assumed there would be a lot of rules to follow in Christianity, just as there is in Islam.

Jeff chuckled when I asked him about the rules and joked, "Okay, don't worry. You'll find out all about them on Sunday!"

Sitting in a Christian church and listening to a sermon for the first time that Sunday morning, I was surprised to hear about nothing but the grace and unconditional love God had for His children. The message was clear—God loved me enough to accept me just the way I was, to send His Son on my behalf to die on a cross and to forgive my sins. I had never heard such a clear story of God's love toward mankind. I couldn't believe my ears! As a former Muslim who always thought one had to obey the rules to please a higher being, this was an incredible message! It liberated me from my greatest fear, that I could not please the God of Christianity, just as I could never satisfy Allah.

As I listened to the message of how much my heavenly Father loved me, I could relate to that love. My earthly father had loved me and sacrificed so much for me, and I knew that his love was real. It was a natural decision to accept my heavenly Father's love as well.

Jesus did not expect me to be perfect, and it was okay—wow, what a miracle! I looked at Jeff and said, "This week, I have experienced many miracles by the hand of Jesus Christ, but this message about God's love is the greatest miracle of all!"

It was July 12, 1987—the date of my new birth, the day I entered into the kingdom of God.

Saving Iraj Erfan

As soon as I became a follower of Jesus Christ, I began to pray for my family's salvation and their safety in Iran, and God answered those prayers in amazing ways.

On July 3, 1988, an airline tragedy occurred over Iranian territorial waters. A US Navy missile cruiser, *USS Vincennes*, mistook a passenger plane for an Iranian fighter jet, and fired at Iran Air Flight 655, killing all 290 people onboard. My father was scheduled to fly Flight 655 that day. He was on his way to the airport when he had the strongest feeling that he needed to turn around. After arriving home, he called his backup pilot to take his place on the flight. Tragically, that pilot and all passengers lost their lives that afternoon. But God saved Iraj Erfan that day, in answer to my prayers for my family's safety.

Later that fall, the eight-year war between Iran and Iraq finally ended. With the war no longer the focus of every government official, it became clear that the incident with my dad blocking the airport runway in 1983 had not been forgotten by the Islamic Republic's secret police. My father was picked up by police guards on his way home from work one day and, without informing anyone, taken straight to Evin Prison.

The authorities brought a summary judgment against him, without giving him a chance to appear in court. None of us had any idea where he was being kept. It was a scary time for our family. We knew that he could spend many years in prison or be executed for his crime. We desperately needed help.

At the time, I had an uncle with a great deal of influence serving in the Iranian Supreme Court. Through his special contacts, he discovered my father's location and miraculously rescued him out of the prison. In the 1980s, Iran was not computerized, and all the legal files and arrest reports in the country were on paper. My father's files were secretly confiscated from the prison warden's office and burned. All evidence against him was destroyed, so the charges were dropped. With the evidence gone, he was even given permission to return to his job with Iran Air.

A few years later, when my father lost his airline job, he, my mother, and my older sister applied to immigrate to the United States. After living in the States for a few years, they became followers of the Lord Jesus Christ and still live here today.

I still reflect on the love of a father that I experienced in those early years—first, the great act of selflessness by my earthly father, who physically set me free from Iran and, second, the unsurpassable love of my heavenly Father, who spiritually set me free from a life of darkness without Him. I am humbled by how much God loved me before I ever knew Him. He clearly saw my future and the calling on my life, and He acted in His power to deliver me from death into life.

I can assure you that our God is not a respecter of persons. His love for us knows no bounds, and His passion for His children is endless. We all are called to great lives of destiny. No matter where you are in life, or whether you believe in Him, He is willing and able to intervene radically to save you. He will set a new direction for you, give men favor toward you, and guide every one of your footsteps before you may even understand His unconditional love for you. He is a good Father.

3

TRYING TO MAKE IT WORK

Time moved quickly. Three years later, I was living in Houston, Texas; had recently become an American citizen; and was working as a chemical engineer at Chevron. I was also an enthusiastic member of the original Lakewood Church, pastored by the late John Osteen. My faith in Christ had grown by leaps and bounds following my college graduation and continued to grow in my new life in Houston.

Then, one Sunday in the summer of 1990, I experienced a new kind of miracle. God spoke to me through a stranger. I was sitting in the front section of church, waiting for the service to begin, when a woman who I had never met before sat down next to me and asked, "Is it okay if I tell you something I believe is from the Lord?"

I was a bit surprised. I had never had a stranger approach me with something to share from God, so with some hesitation, I replied, "Yes, of course."

"Young man," she said, "I know you will be a wealthy man one day. When I saw you walking into the church this morning, I saw money falling out of your pockets every place you walked, and the money was filling the church! God will bless you mightily, and you will bless the church one day."

I didn't know what to say. I was dumbfounded. Wow—what a great word of encouragement! "I will receive that by faith," I finally answered her. But later that day, when I looked at the reality of my financial situation, even after receiving two raises at work, her prophesy seemed far-fetched, to say the least. I was barely making enough money to pay my bills, and the idea of making so much money that it would fall out of my pockets seemed far out of the realm of possibility. I had a lot to learn about God's kind of faith.

The Best Money Plan

Before going on with the story, I need to share what happened a month earlier. During a Wednesday night service, the pastor had been teaching on the concept of tithes and offerings in the church. Now, for those of you unfamiliar with the concept, tithes and offerings are the basis by which Christians financially support the church with a certain percentage of their income. They are not an invention of the church but a biblical teaching of the Word of God. The biblical tithe is 10 percent of a person's income, which might seem like a lot, but I saw it as though I had the remaining 90 percent of the money to use as I pleased.

Frankly, until that night, I had never heard a biblical teaching on finances. Listening to God's Word on the subject stirred my heart. I wanted to obey Him, to put God first in everything in my life, especially in my finances. However, there was one little problem—I didn't have the money to do anything. My bills totaled more than my income, and to give 10 percent of it back to building God's kingdom appeared to be a financial impossibility. I was perplexed. Should I trust God, or should I look at my checkbook balance and give it more time?

God won the argument that night, so now came the tough part—how was I going to do it? I remember putting all my bills in a stack and deciding which ones I could delay by a month without getting into too much trouble. I finally settled on two bills I could pass on for the time being and placed them on the bottom of the stack. Taking a deep breath, I wrote my first check to the church for 10 percent of my income. As I wrote out the check, a sense of deep joy and real fear came over me. I was both elated and terrified. This always happens when you do something challenging, right? I believed I had done the right thing, but I still had a nagging fear saying, *This won't last long!*

> *I knew that I was not the best engineer in the company. I worked hard, but I was not being rewarded because I had tremendous merit. To me, it was clear that God and God alone had rewarded me for putting Him first. I gave Him all the credit for the blessing.*

Just two weeks later, I was called into my boss's office, and he surprised me with a 10 percent raise—exactly the amount I had committed to God! A few weeks after that, another 12 percent was added to my salary. It all seemed too impossible to believe—two raises in one month? Who gets two raises in a month?

I should have known that the same God who had performed all those miracles in the first week of my salvation was quite capable of giving me a double raise if He wanted to. I knew that I was not the best engineer in the company. I worked hard, but I was not being rewarded because I had tremendous merit. To me, it was clear that God and God alone had rewarded me for putting Him first. I gave Him all the credit for the blessing.

Just a few weeks after I began to tithe, I received the word from the woman at church about the tremendous financial blessing, that money would be falling out of my pockets and that it would bless the church! If the Lord wanted to get my attention, He certainly succeeded!

My Dream of Owning a Business

When a word of encouragement comes from the Lord, other confirmations will follow. The following month, I attended a meeting with a small gathering of believers listening to a message of a traveling evangelist. In the middle of his message, the evangelist looked directly at me and told me that he had a word for me that he believed was from the Lord. This was the second word given to me by a stranger!

This evangelist told me that he believed I would travel around the globe for both business and ministry. He could see me hopping from one country to another helping others in their business and faith. It was the first time I ever received a clear picture of my calling. God would use the world of commerce to bless me and, more importantly, to bless His church.

Remember, ever since I was very young, I dreamed of owning a business of my own. Since becoming a Christian, I realized that financial blessings of a business could be used in a dynamic way to expand Christ's message around the world. Now, the evangelist was giving me a word of encouragement that God was going to use me exactly as I had dreamed! One day, I would travel around the world to run my own business, and I would be used by God at the same time! Could this really happen?

Later that year, I met a man who was fulfilling that same calling. He was an Iranian Christian businessman who had a very successful rug dealership in Tulsa, Oklahoma. In addition to pastoring an Iranian church in Tulsa, he founded Bible studies for converted Muslims in Dallas and Oklahoma City. He was both a successful businessman and a minister of the gospel. We became friends, and I looked up to him as a model example of the life I desired to live in Christ.

I was so excited! I was also still very young in the Lord, and I saw this as a new challenge to rise to the occasion. If my Iranian friend could do it all, then I could be the man to fulfill God's promises. I had no idea that God worked to fulfill His own promises in ways unlike our own! "*'For my thoughts are not your thoughts, neither are your ways my ways,' declares the Lord. 'As the heavens are higher than the earth, so are my ways higher than your ways, and my thoughts than your thoughts'*" (Isaiah 55:8–9).

I had so much to learn! No one warned me that God's promises are often accompanied by long training times and that the heavenly message would be, *Mani, you must wait.*

In the summer of 1990, when I received those words of encouragement from the Lord, it never occurred to me that it would take twelve years before I would see the first signs of this promised success in business! Twelve years—and a great deal of hard work—before I began living out my dreams. Before I started my two businesses, UNICAT and IRA Consulting, I had made many unsuccessful attempts to fulfill God's promises in my own strength. With multiple false starts and failures, I tried to accomplish what I knew was my destiny with my own hands and according to my own timetable, but God knew I was not yet prepared.

Two Seconds from Death

Becoming a distributor in Amway, setting up a kiosk to sell "talking" balloons in the mall, helping a Christian friend develop a jet engine fuel additive in the back of his garage, becoming a founding member of a new multilevel marketing company, selling meteoric rock as a next-generation humidity trap, setting up shop as a manufacturer of a Christian clothing line for men—I invested my limited resources and my youthful energy in companies and ideas that I thought would lead me to the promised land of success. I look back at that time and laugh when I think of God's patience with me.

I was young, energetic, and hopeful, so there was no shortage of effort. In the early 1990s, when I was trying to build an Amway distributorship, I drove two or three days a week to San Antonio from Houston. I would leave from work at 4:00 P.M. and arrive in San Antonio at 8:00 P.M., conduct my meetings, and then get right back on the road at midnight and arrive back at my apartment around 4:00 A.M.—just in time to grab an hour of sleep, take a shower, and go back to work that morning.

In one of these late-night drives back to Houston, God supernaturally saved me from a fatal car accident. It was around 3:00 A.M., and I was on a two-lane highway near Columbus, Texas. I must have fallen asleep at the wheel, because I drifted over to the opposite lane, driving straight into oncoming traffic. All I remember was that I woke up, grabbed the wheel, and, without panicking, steered the car back over to the right lane. Then, I seemed to hear the word *count* in my head, so I counted: one second, two seconds, and—*whoosh*—a semitrailer raced passed me going in the opposite direction blaring its horn! All the while, I was driving sixty miles an hour.

When I could finally pull over, my heart was beating a thousand beats a minute! How close I came to death—a mere two seconds! I was certain God had sent an angel to save me. I wasn't the one who woke up just in time, I wasn't the one who calmly took control of the steering wheel as my Honda Civic sped down the highway at sixty miles an hour—some unseen force had taken over and calmly steered my car back into the right lane to avoid a head-on collision with that semitrailer. God had been looking after me and, once more, I owed my very life to Him.

Crazy Business Ventures

I must admit, even after that incident, I continued to invest in crazy business ventures, one of which was partnering with a jet-engine fuel additive company. How naïve I was about the complex world of business aviation and the staggering number of regulations necessary to keep airline passengers safe. That venture was short-lived.

I even signed a contract, along with two other investors, with a rather dubious man who claimed that a meteorite had landed on his property in north Texas, had been tested, and was the most amazing hygroscopic material known to man (by that, I mean a humidity trap). I don't know who was crazier, my partners and I, who branded and packaged the rocks and sold them to stores nationwide, or the 2,500 people who actually bought the stuff and put the units into their refrigerators. That lasted just a little longer than the jet-engine experiment.

I went from one venture to another, and the list of my failures started to grow. I didn't just lose money in these strange deals, my ego was shattered and my self-confidence dropped to an all-time low. I knew that God had made a promise, but I thought it was up to me to find a way to fulfill it. I remember my close friends and family members skeptically asking, "Is this a Mani idea or a God idea?" I could never truly answer that question. My response was usually, "It's just a good idea!" But through it all, I never stopped believing that God does not lie and that the failures were mine, not His.

I never stopped believing that God does not lie and that the failures were mine, not His.

During the ten years of missteps and failed starts, I learned something very valuable about myself and God. I learned that I had a hard head and, no matter how bad I fell or how miserable my failure, I was still able to get up, brush the dirt off, and go after my dream. In addition, I learned that although God was patient with me, He had no intention of sharing His glory and success with me or any other man. If I was going to succeed as He promised, it would be for His strength and for His glory and in His perfect timing. I needed to wait for the God idea.

4

DON'T LET EMOTIONS RULE YOU

Sales. The sky is the limit in sales. The harder you work, the more money you make.

After just a year at Chevron, I left my engineering job for a lucrative position as a salesman for Haldor Topsøe, a Danish catalyst company. Because you will hear a lot about catalyst in my story, let me explain it in a little more detail right now. Catalyst is a chemical product, either a solid or a liquid, that promotes a set of reactions necessary for a chemical or refinery operation. Catalyst increases the rate of activity in chemical reactions and, therefore, increases an industrial plant's production. I have spent most of my adult life developing or selling catalyst products for oil, gas, and petrochemical industries. It is the vehicle that brought me so much success in business.

Why did I enter the world of chemical sales? Because I realized that my personality and interests were better suited to selling chemical products than developing them! It is so vitally important to find out where our strengths are if we are called to the world of commerce.

This was my first true sales job, selling catalyst products to the oil industry, and I was good at it. Joining the company at just twenty-three years old, I was the new kid on the block, without any prior sales experience. I was assigned the "last ditch" sales territory, which was a patchwork of twenty-six clients from Georgia to Alaska. My colleagues chuckled when they told me that any potential customer who did not want to buy from Topsøe was thrown in a pot and presented to me as a client base. I would be lucky, they said, to sell in my territory.

So what did I do? My first year at Topsøe, I traveled almost nonstop for forty-two weeks and built incredible relationships with my clients. I gained their trust and, within two years, turned the hodgepodge, underperforming territory into the best-producing region in the entire company, with over $6.5 million in sales. I was known to take on the most difficult accounts, and I had the highest level of respect from the upper management. The following year, I was promoted to a sales management position.

The problem was that I knew I was supposed to be in my own business one day, and I didn't believe that staying at Topsøe would ever lead me to my ultimate destination. Additionally, Topsøe was a European company with a more socialistic view of employee compensation, trying to keep all employees within a certain range of income regardless of their performance. I knew that I was capped financially, and no matter how hard I worked in the future, I would never reach my financial potential. Even though I was very successful at Topsøe, there was a financial ceiling I could not break through.

Just as I was considering what move I should make in my career, I received an enticing job offer from a small industrial waste recycling company in Houston.

"Come work for me, Mani," the owner offered. "I'm going to give you a great sales region. It will be the hardest you've ever worked, but if you can reach one million dollars in sales in one year, your commission will be 10 percent. Work hard, Mani, and you can reach that $100,000 sales bonus!"

A $100,000 sales commission! If I could reach one million dollars in sales within one year, I would receive that $100,000 bonus above my salary. Boy, was I interested!

Still, the decision to leave Topsøe wasn't easy. It was a large, prestigious company with a nice office location, high profile products, and a professionally run enterprise with global respect. In contrast, the new offer came from a small company with dirty offices in the old warehouse district of Houston, a very small staff, and minimal job security. Worst of all, the product was not the creation of new and exciting chemical catalyst but the recycling of industrial waste!

I do want to interject one positive thing here: Although it isn't glamorous, industrial waste recycling is beneficial to both industry and the environment. The recycling operation consists of extracting renewable resources like metals from the waste generated from many industrial operations. Instead of the reusable resources just being dumped in an industrial landfill, they are extracted and reused in other industrial processes. Everybody wins.

When I received a warning that the top management at the new company did not always operate with the highest level of integrity, I was really stumped. Why had I been so intrigued by this offer? Why in the world had I taken this leap of faith and changed jobs? Simply because I had seen the very real possibility of fulfilling my dreams of financial success and independence one day. I still wasn't sure if this was what the Lord had in mind, but I wanted to take the risk.

I made that leap of faith in September 1993. Everyone told me I was absolutely crazy to leave my job at Topsøe for the new position. In fact, I wasn't even offered a higher salary to join the new company. But there was that enticing reward, if I could reach just one million dollars in sales in a year, that $100,000 sales bonus would be mine.

I knew nothing about the industrial waste recycling industry, but I was determined to make a go at it. And boom—I hit a brick wall from the very beginning. My coworkers said that my opportunities were nil. They would tell me that all the main contracts were already under other sales people and that they didn't know why I had been hired.

Within thirty days, I was overwhelmed and ready to head back to Topsøe. I saw no path to success—my peers didn't want me, the scope of the work was enormous, and I had absolutely no one to show me the ropes.

Nothing of Value Comes Without Risk

Topsøe had assured me they would welcome me back. What should I do? I wasn't the kind of person who moved backward; I always tracked forward with great zeal. If I went back, it would be admitting defeat.

In the end, the Lord reminded me that nothing of value comes without sacrifice and risk. Without risk, there is no potential for true reward, but with all risk comes possible loss and defeat. I had to accept those facts. I had risked it all. I had to see it through.

With zero guidance from others, I turned to the Lord for His guidance and plans. Then I ventured into an area where no one at the company had gone before—seeking international customers. All the salesmen were focused on the lucrative United States business, and no one had considered the overseas market. The logic in the 1990s was that overseas companies were not as environmentally conscious as the

United States and were not interested in contracting a company to handle their industrial waste.

What I did was a complete shot in the dark. There were books in the home office that listed every chemical company in the world. I simply took the information and sent out faxes to every one of them, over one thousand in all, introducing the company and what we could do to save them money. Yes, this was in the 1990s—the era of faxes and pagers. We had not yet graduated to the Internet, emails, and cell phones! In a matter of weeks, I had thirty active sales opportunities from companies all over the globe.

Was that first year at industrial recycling frightening? You bet it was! But I worked harder than I had ever worked in my life. Finally, I reached my million-dollar sales quota for just one year. I was beyond excited. I'll never forget it.

At the end of that successful year, I stood in the CEO's wood-paneled office. He sat down at his cluttered desk and avoided eye contact with me.

"Mani," he confessed guiltily, "you're a great salesman. I knew you would be successful if you came to work for me, but I never thought you could reach one million dollars in sales in one year. I can't pay you a $100,000 commission—not even close. We just don't have the money. The most I can come up with is maybe $20,000."

I stormed out of his office. I was livid! I paced back and forth in the empty warehouse muttering to myself. I had worked so hard to reach that goal, sacrificing time and family interests to prove I could do it. I received the first big financial upset of my life.

My emotions were all over the place: I was angry, I was afraid, I was filled with regret that I had ever taken this job. I had made a big mistake and, in spite of experiencing a miraculous success against all odds that year, my entire effort and the huge risk I had taken were in vain. My pockets had been cleaned out, and I was ready to fight back.

Thank God I am a Christian and that I had someone outside of myself to turn to during this wretched time. I cried out to the Lord in anger and frustration, "I'm quitting today, Lord! I don't know why I came to this horrible place, but this is the last day I will be here!"

"I Am Your Supply"

The words I heard God speak to my heart were almost as shocking as the words my employer had spoken to me just hours earlier.

He said to me, "Mani, don't leave this job."

"But, Lord, they deceived me. They stole from me. I earned that money."

"This is the way of the world, Mani. The world is not your supply. This company is not your supply. I am your supply. I want you to stay here and trust me. Learn all you can about business from them. It is like another college degree for you. Trust me for your prosperity."

Then the Lord said one final thing that was probably the hardest for me to hear that day: "I want you to be a servant to the management, Mani. Learn as a diligent servant. Work for them with integrity and honor them in spite of your feelings. Represent my highest standards, and you will be rewarded in due time."

The Lord said one final thing that was probably the hardest for me to hear that day: "I want you to be a servant to the management, Mani.... Work for them with integrity and honor them in spite of your feelings. Represent my highest standards, and you will be rewarded in due time."

Looking back, I can see tremendous wisdom in God's counsel. My boss was an experienced businessman who could apprentice me in the field of recycling and teach me the trade. These words from the Lord anchored me in that work environment for nearly seven more years. Instead of letting my emotions rule my decisions, I surrendered to the will of God for my life at that time. I remained diligent and never really complained.

In a few years, I built an $11 million international business, which hardly existed at the time of my hiring, and I became the most successful sales representative the company had ever had. I was promoted time and again, and, in my final years there, I was basically running the company and making $200,000 a year, which was substantial back in 1999.

Most importantly, I learned the business of industrial metal recycling, and built strong business relationships and friendships around the globe. Later, when I was on my own, I developed new trade with these contacts. By God's grace, I have made millions of dollars in profit over the years, far more than the $100,000 I had been denied back in 1994. The Lord paid me back many times over for my trouble.

God honors His children. He protects us and has our back. Don't give in to negative circumstances and situations in your life and business. Don't let anger and resentment rule your decisions. Anchor yourself in the truth God has planted in you.

When you take risks for God, or just take a risk to create a better life for you and your family, things don't always pan out exactly the way you plan. However, if you trust in God's faithfulness, and if you stay the course in disheartening situations, God will bring out good. You will learn, you will grow, you will be better equipped for challenges in the future, and you will be stronger. You can never figure out how God will bless you in the future for sticking to His counsel and not your own mind.

Don't give in, but go on.

5

THE IMPOSSIBLE BECOMES POSSIBLE

During the late 1990s, China was abuzz with trading companies and manufacturers that were extremely eager to find markets in the West for their products. They went any length to make a deal. The international sales unit I developed for the industrial recycling company took me across the globe, and mainland China became one of my regular client destinations. During one business trip, a trading company approached me about selling Chinese-made catalyst for the oil industry through my employer in the United States.

The idea was unique and piqued my interest. I knew from my experience at TopsØe that the catalyst business was very competitive, and there were some large companies in the United States and Europe that had pretty tight control of the market. But China had no players in the catalyst game, and some Chinese manufacturers wanted a chance to enter. Although the idea was intriguing, I brushed it off as too crazy to consider. Still, I could not get the concept out of my mind.

The following year, in 1998, I was in China on business and had an unforgettable encounter with a Chinese businessman and his team. I traveled from Hong Kong to Guangzhou for a one-day meeting with an industrial plant owner who wanted to know more about our recycling company. I found my way to his cramped office in a high-rise building in the crowded city. Once there, I was startled by the direction the meeting took. It had nothing to do with industrial waste.

After initial Chinese formalities and the customary offer of green tea, the businessman placed a large catalog in front of me and said, in broken English, "Anything you see in this catalog, I can find and sell it to you. Just point to it, and I will get you a price!"

Skeptical of his boastfulness, I opened the book and found myself staring at the granddaddy of all catalogs. Clothing, cosmetics, chemicals, home appliances, electronics, industrial tools, machinery, cars, tractors, buses, planes—yes, you read it right, *planes,* and I mean military planes—guns, tanks, and air-to-air rockets—yep, it was all there. I could not believe my eyes. This guy was telling me I could buy missiles and tanks out of a catalog!

I tried to collect myself and then remembered the catalyst inquiry I had received during my last trip to China. So I asked him if he had any catalyst that he could offer.

He answered emphatically, "Oh, yes, just look up the section with chemicals. It's all there."

And there it was. Nestled in between the military hardware and the sports equipment was a list of catalyst products with pictures and chemical ingredients for the buyer to consider.

Immediately, catalyst ideas began whirling around in my brain. I thought to myself, *Maybe this is why the Lord wouldn't let me get this catalyst idea out of my head. I am being offered this whole new business opportunity. Do I need to get more serious about it? Was this the God idea I had been waiting for?*

Whoa, wait a minute! If this was a God idea, it was one of the craziest ones I had ever heard! It was like a suicide mission! Selling industrial catalyst to modern refineries and chemical plants was monumentally more complex than recycling metals and industrial waste. If I was crazy enough to launch into the catalyst business, I would have to compete against multibillion-dollar companies with worldwide offices, decades of brand exposure and experience, research facilities, marketing budgets, and dozens of sales people.

If that was not hard enough to overcome, all the worldwide refineries and chemical companies, such as Exxon, Chevron, and British Petroleum, would be my clients and certainly would not risk buying a critical product like catalyst from a no-name company. It seemed unfathomable to me that one of these international oil companies would take a chance by buying catalyst from a startup venture and risking plant failure that could cost them millions of dollars a day in lost revenue.

So why couldn't I get this idea out of my head? I tried not to think about it, but I tossed and turned many nights, considering all the possibilities. Then, in late 1998, two of the smaller catalyst companies in North America were sold to larger competitors. This meant that there were only three companies left selling catalyst to the entire oil industry. I heard rumblings that the oil manufacturers were not happy about it. Catalyst prices were soaring because of lack of competition. Well, if there was ever a time to begin a new catalyst company, it was now.

Still, I was beyond overwhelmed! There was no way I could see myself starting this enterprise all on my own. I had very few options open to me, so I decided to approach my employer and pitch the idea to him. His initial reaction was very positive, and he told me to give him a little time to work something out. A few months passed, and when I approached him again, his response was the same—to wait a few more months. By this time, six months had passed, and it was already 1999. I was feeling very uneasy that the window of opportunity was going to close on the business and my willingness to even consider it.

Finally, a God Idea

I was convinced of one thing by now: This idea was too big and too ambitious to be from me! A seed had been planted in my heart. This was a God idea, and the Lord had His hands squarely on the project. I had believed for years that when an idea or project was far bigger than I could meet with my own abilities and resources, then God himself had a divine purpose for it. He wants to be glorified when the impossible comes to pass.

> *I had believed for years that when an idea or project was far bigger than I could meet with my own abilities and resources, then God himself had a divine purpose for it. He wants to be glorified when the impossible comes to pass.*

Now, my boss was still dragging his feet, so I began to think that perhaps his reluctance was God's will. Maybe God didn't want me to mess up this business idea by bringing in the wrong partner. But now I was back to square one: Who could help me launch this new business? I couldn't comprehend going it alone.

I am sure that when most people are about to launch a new business venture, they have a sense of excitement and fear. And the bigger the risk, the more frightening the experience. I can attest that, in my case, the fear was way more prominent than the excitement. I was totally overcome by it. When I stopped to think about what I was contemplating, the enormity of the task was simply overwhelming. I would often talk to God and, without being irreverent, ask Him if He was out of His mind. Did He realize what He was asking me to do?

"Lord, you want me, Mani Erfan, with minimal resources and only three years of experience selling industrial catalyst, to start an international catalyst company? You are asking me to compete with multinational, billion-dollar companies in Europe and the United States. You want me to go before Exxon, Shell, and Chevron and convince them to buy critical products, vital to running their plants, from a no-name company with a staff of one, no facility of my own, and no research and development? And, Lord, I have no one to support me through it! I am completely alone in this project!"

The questions continued to spin around in my head and to spill out in earnest prayer to the God of heaven.

In addition, I had the weight of the company I worked for on my shoulders. The recycling business was going through some tough times financially, and I was needed at my job more than ever. Because I was the one generating the highest sales volume, my boss actually depended on me to cover the bills at the end of the month. I felt the weight and responsibility of an owner without the actual benefits of ownership. Sometimes, I just wanted to leave the job, forget about owning a business, and find a less stressful working environment—just stop the struggle and let go of my dream once and for all.

Four more months passed, and I made one last pitch to my employer. I was just hoping he would say yes so that I could dump the project on him and not have to do it on my own. This time, the answer was a definite no. He was not going to invest in a catalyst company after all.

Oh, how I wanted to drop the whole idea! But I couldn't deny the still, small voice inside me that kept saying, *Leave your job, start this business, and I will be with you. Put your trust in Me!*" Now, it had become an issue of obedience, of having reverential fear and respect for the Lord. The decision had to be made.

I'm Not Going It Alone

During this time, I became friends with a Christian businessman named Jim McKimmy, who attended the same church in Alvin, Texas. One of Jim's business ventures was with a company that sold catalyst. By the time I got the courage to share my crazy idea with him, he was already in a different business, becoming very successful very fast. His initial reaction was startling. He actually thought starting a catalyst company was a good idea, but he made it clear that he had absolutely no time to invest in the venture himself. I wasn't surprised by this, because I knew Jim was fielding as many as a hundred calls a day for his own business.

Near the end of 1999, Jim called me. I don't remember the exact conversation, but I can tell you that what Jim shared that day both thrilled and frightened me. He had prayed about the new catalyst venture, and the Lord had told him to help me with the business, to devote a portion of his time and his financial resources to launching the company.

Now this was becoming serious! I would no longer be alone. I had some startup capital, but I was still afraid. There were monumental obstacles in front of me: We had just crossed off two of these giants from the list, but so many remained. I needed more confirmation before I was willing to jump off the cliff.

Not long after our conversation, Jim and I attended an oil and gas trade show in Houston. Jim had his own booth, and I was representing my employer. While hanging around in the booth talking, a Chinese businessman named Eric Lui walked over to us and asked Jim about his business. As he spoke, I could hear God's voice once again. *Mani, you need to get to know this man.*

So I stepped out in faith. "Eric, do you know anything about the catalyst business?"

He responded no but said he would be happy to find out what he could for me. I gave him a list of questions and products that I wanted to see, and he asked for several weeks to get the information together. Little did I know that the wheels of destiny were set in motion that day. I had officially embarked on an irreversible course to start a multimillion-dollar success called UNICAT Catalyst Technologies, Inc.

Several weeks later, I sat across from Eric at a Chinese restaurant in Houston, looking through bags of catalyst samples, asking questions, and reading pages of information. By the close of that meeting, I knew I had found the right person to overcome the third largest obstacle facing me: how to secure the right products from China with a trustworthy agent who could help me navigate the many manufacturers there.

Miracles Beyond Measure

It is difficult, in just one chapter, to share all the miracles and the amazing favor that God showed Jim and me through our relationship with Eric Lui and the company he represented. With all the new opportunities suddenly opening up for us, we decided that Jim should travel to China to meet face-to-face with the nine directors of the Northern Industrial Group of China. All Chinese businesses are ultimately controlled by the government, and these directors were personally responsible for hundreds of manufacturing plants and 25 million workers in northern China!

All eyes were focused on Jim as he presented our business plan—to use Chinese suppliers to manufacture catalyst products we would sell worldwide. When he finished, the finance director looked Jim straight in the eye, smiled, and said, "We don't give an open line of credit to anyone, but we are going to give one to you."

Jim was shocked and asked the man, "Why would you do that for me after just one hour of conversation? You don't even know me or my partner."

The director's answer had to be from heaven itself.

"You are going to be my American son. (He was barely ten years older than Jim.) I have always wanted to have an American friend. When I look in your eyes, I see someone I can trust. So now, if you tell me you need five million, you got it. If it is ten million, you got it."

"What if, in a couple of years, I tell you I need twenty-five million?"

The response came back quickly, "Jim, an open line of credit means whatever you need. That is why it is an open line."

We are certain this was God's go-ahead for UNICAT. How else can anyone explain a multimillion-dollar line of credit interest-free, with indefinite repayment terms and no written contract extended to a small, unknown US company with no financial history?

It was astounding! God had surely intervened! Who in the world would give someone an unlimited line of credit within the first thirty minutes of meeting them? God had given us unbelievable favor, and it continued. We received an interest-free line of credit worth millions of dollars with flexible payment terms, a dedicated staff that worked diligently—and still works today, two decades later—on UNICAT's behalf, favor with Chinese manufacturing plants, and protection from larger US and European competitors who tried to disrupt our business product pipeline. Eric and his team bestowed one favor after another to get our business launched successfully.

We are certain this was God's go-ahead for UNICAT. How else can anyone explain a multimillion-dollar line of credit interest-free, with indefinite repayment terms and no written contract extended to a small, unknown US company with no financial history? Only the hand of the Lord could have brought us such a miracle of favor!

"I Am a God of Exponential Returns"

Believe it or not, even in the face of all these miracles, I still hadn't resigned from my job! We can be such stubborn creatures before a patient and giving God. Even though the Lord had sorted out the financial and the supply side of the business, I was still afraid to take the leap, to resign from my position, to give up my comfortable salary, and to officially start the company. I was afraid of change, afraid to risk financial failure, and afraid of rejection from any potential customers. It weighed so heavily on me that I refused to make a decision, even though I knew what God wanted me to do. I was running out of excuses.

Several times, I gathered up the courage to resign, but each time, I would get a call from the company owner, and he would give me a promotion in income and position. One day, when I decided to resign, my boss gave me a $20,000 raise. I knew this was not a coincidence. Even Satan was on hand to keep me from my destiny. I still did not have the courage or faith to leave and get on the road to my future. God was beyond patient with me!

Finally, one day, I believe the Lord asked me a very direct question: *Mani, you think you are such a high roller making all this money, but what if you were to give me a double or triple tithe out of the money you are making right now? What could you do for me and my church?* I thought about it and realized that $40,000 or even $60,000 would not have the kind of impact I wanted to have in the kingdom of God by reaching Muslims in the Middle East.

Then God spoke a Word that has stayed with me to this day and will remain with me until I graduate to heaven: *Mani, you are trading your days and weeks for mere pennies, but if you trust Me, I will help you make hundreds and thousands of dollars in mere minutes. I am a God of exponential returns.*

It was April 2000, almost two years after God had first placed the idea of a catalyst company in my heart, when I sensed the powerful presence of the Holy Spirit. Things had been getting unbearable in the office, and I was working seventy to eighty hours a week to help my employer stay afloat. I was sitting at my desk when I heard clearly from the Lord: *Mani, leave your job today. Pack up your bags and resign right now. This company is dying, and you can't save it. If you don't leave, the opportunity and the door I have opened for you will close.*

I couldn't fight Him anymore. I knew I'd heard from God above, and He was not kidding. The time to leave was right then. No more excuses and no more room for hesitation. I closed my computer, packed up my briefcase, walked to the human resources office, and dropped a bombshell: "I am leaving, and this is my last day."

I apologized for not giving them an advance notice, but I couldn't stay a moment longer. The human resources manager was shocked, and tried to talk me into staying a little longer and meeting with the owner, but I knew that would only tempt me to stay, and that was not an option anymore.

I rushed out of there as if the building was on fire. Heading toward home, I cried and yet I sensed a great feeling of joy that comes from pure obedience. I had no idea what tomorrow had in store for me. So many questions remained unanswered. How was I going to convince multibillion-dollar companies to buy my product? How was I going to run a company since I had no experience? Was I going to succeed or was this going to be another one of my failed ventures? I could not think clearly, and my heart was pounding, but still I sensed a great peace and the awesome presence of His Holy Spirit around and within me. I knew I was exactly in the right place at that moment of my life.

The journey had begun! I had been standing on the edge of the cliff for several months, even years, afraid to take that final decisive step. But I had leaped off. I was flying, and I could feel the wind of God all around me. I was terrified and overjoyed at the same time. The feeling you get when you jump out of an airplane with a parachute—it is indescribable. I knew God had me in His arms, and I had the parachute on, but I could not help seeing the ground rushing up to meet me. Now it was time to face the daunting task of walking out my faith, and seeing one of the craziest business ideas ever conceived in the industrial world through to the end.

Still, in that moment, I could hear the Lord speaking down from heaven, "You go there, my son. You look great flying out there."

6

DON'T DESPISE THE DAY OF SMALL BEGINNINGS

"Who dares despise the day of small things…?"
—Zechariah 4:10

No business ever starts as a large enterprise from day one. No church ever begins with members in the thousands at its first service. It was no different for me. The first week of the business started with a bang, but not necessarily the good kind.

My previous employer did not take the news that I was leaving too well, and I quickly heard from his lawyers. I was going to be sued unless I signed a noncompete agreement with them immediately. I found myself sitting in a lawyer's office with Jim, trying to figure out what to do next. As if I was not scared enough already, now I had this to worry about.

I can remember standing in the shower that first week, overcome by waves of fear, feeling lost in a sea of uncertainty. Then I heard the voice of the Lord speaking in my heart, *Thank you!*

"Thank me, Lord? Why are you thanking *me*? I should be thanking You for all the good things You have done in my life." I went on thanking Him for everything I could think of, and then I heard Him say again, *Thank you!*

"For what, Lord? What did I do for you?"

Thank you for your obedience, son. Because of your obedience, I can glorify my name in the catalyst business, where no one knows me or knows of me. You have given me a new mountain in which I can raise up my name.

I was overwhelmed and shaken. I was so thankful for those words. I knew I had made the right decision and, regardless of the difficult circumstances I faced in those early days, His words were a continual source of comfort to me.

The threat of a lawsuit never materialized, and the business got off to a good start. We actually were successful with our first sales call to our client Giant Refining. The transaction went through easily and without any glitches. I thought to myself, *Wait a minute, this crazy idea could actually work!* I was so excited. It was not a big sale, but it made money, and I saw it as encouraging confirmation from the Lord that success would follow.

Shortly afterward, Jim came to me with another word he believed the Lord had spoken. "Mani, it's going to take two years before we experience a real breakthrough."

Two years? No way. "Look, Jim, we just closed our first deal, and it was quick. It won't take two years. I am sure of it!"

Well, you can guess how long it took for us to experience success—two years. What God left out of this word to Jim was what we—more specifically, I—had to go through to get there. He never mentioned the hundreds of rejections, failed promises, disheartening news, and overwhelmingly negative responses I would face going from one meeting to another in those first two years. I lost count of how many no's I heard. I never failed so many times in my entire life.

We would secure an order, and then it would be snatched from us. Someone would express an interest, and then they would change their mind and buy from one of our larger competitors. Debt and frustration was the currency of the day.

"He Who Is Faithful Will Do It"

I cried many times, I quit numerous times, and I can't even count how many times I got angry with God for putting this wild business idea in my heart and mind. I chided myself for believing it was God who guided this ride to bankruptcy. I remember working on a business relationship with a client in Aruba for an entire year. The potential for the business was enormous, and the manager of the plant was a friend of Jim's. We had filled one small order for them in our first year of business, and now we were working on a contract that would make the company close to $400,000 annually.

The product was tested, and the test was a great success. The price was low, and our customer was happy with it. It seemed there was no way the deal could fall through. Out of left field came the bad news. The week that the large order was to be placed, the company was sold. The new owners had their own regulations that prevented them from purchasing from new entities or small companies, and we were both. All that work came to nothing!

The same thing happened with a firm in Puerto Rico during that same period. I can't begin to tell you how disheartening these losses were for me. There seemed to be no reason for going on.

I would sit there and wonder, *Why would the Lord allow these things to happen?* Jim and I prayed, and we honored God with our lives, so why weren't we succeeding? Such bad news was the norm rather than the exception during those first two years. We operated on a shoestring budget. I would travel and stay in the cheapest hotels, trying to keep our expenses as low as possible. It was hard to see Jim pour money into the company with no return; I felt responsible for his losses, and no matter what I tried, I could not get things rolling.

My life during those first two years was a mixture of enormous frustration and undeniable peace, jam-packed together in the same bottle. On one hand, I was overwhelmed by the negative results of the company; on the other hand, I had an inner sense of joy and peace, knowing I had obeyed God's call. Beyond working my tail off, I ultimately was not responsible for what lay ahead in my life. I had to let the ultimate responsibility rest on the One who had called me to this venture.

> *Let us hold fast the confession of our hope without wavering, for He who promised is faithful.* (Hebrews 10:23 NASB)

> *He who calls you is faithful, who also will do it.*
> (1 Thessalonians 5:24 NKJV)

When the going was especially rough, Jim would remind me that I was experiencing God's "peace that passes understanding" (see Philippians 4:7), when, for all practical purposes, I should have had no peace at all. That is the truth. As I look back, I realize that peace is not the absence of adversity and problems in our lives; it is the very presence of confidence that we are operating in His perfect will in the midst of difficult circumstances. It is the surrender of our will, when we know we cannot do anything more than what we are doing, and the remainder rests in His good hands. Having done all we can, we simply stand on His will and His goodness. (See Ephesians 6:13.)

Peace is not the absence of adversity and problems in our lives; it is the very presence of confidence that we are operating in His perfect will in the midst of difficult circumstances. It is the surrender of our will, when we know we cannot do anything more than what we are doing, and the remainder rests in His good hands.

Now that I have experienced years of success and prosperity, it seems that I no longer experience the same depth of inner peace I'd felt during those early years. It seems that, with the confidence that accompanies success, we lose a bit of our surrendered will and complete abandonment of self that comes with pure obedience. We sort of become the captain of our own ship, and take the wheel back into our own hands.

In those early days, the smallest success seemed like an enormous victory, and the faintest good news was received with great joy. I was content with little, and I certainly did not have much, but the Lord took care of my family incredibly well.

In early December 2000, I started complaining to God that I did not have enough money to buy Christmas gifts for my family. I had never been in that situation before. After moaning and groaning to the Lord one morning at work, I left that evening to go home, and told my family to be prepared for slim pickings under the Christmas tree that year. The next morning, when I walked into my office, I saw a $1,000 check from my partner on my desk. I quickly walked to his office and asked what the check was for.

Jim said that he had been praying the night before, and the Lord told him to give me a one thousand-dollar check for Christmas and to tell me to stop complaining!

Moments like these led me to believe that my Father in heaven had my back. Miracles do not need to be large or spectacular to change lives. God does not always work on a grand scale or in "parting the sea" moments. A thousand-dollar check from a friend at the perfect time was as great a miracle as the $2,000 that appeared in my bank account in my college days. Despite the drastic reduction in my salary those first two years, the Lord provided for my every need. We also continued to give to the Lord's work, seeding His church and obeying His word.

God's Word says to give, and we wanted above all else to be obedient. It became easier as time went on. God took care of my family, and we truly never suffered or did without anything we needed. It was a great miracle during those early days, how God took care of my family, and I have never truly figured out how He did it.

Destiny Traps

At this stage of my story, I want to share something very important. During the first two years of working to make UNICAT a reality, I had several opportunities to quit, and join other companies that wanted to hire me as a partner or a high-paid sales manager. I had six-figure offers come my way, with very attractive benefits. They were quite tempting, especially because I wasn't making much money, and there seemed to be no light at the end of the UNICAT tunnel. But I recognized these for what they were—destiny traps.

Destiny traps are options that the enemy puts in front of us when the going gets rough; falling into them is following the path of least resistance. It is Satan's attempt to lead us to an alternate future, which is not our ultimate destiny, not part of God's plan for our lives. During difficult seasons, these options pop up in our businesses, marriages, education, and whatever area we are obeying the Father. For me, these lucrative jobs offers were just that—traps. I am thankful the Holy Spirit gave me enough wisdom to stay the course. And I felt responsible both to God and to Jim, who had invested half a million dollars to launch UNICAT.

By July 2001, I was truly ready to give up. I cried out in frustration, "Lord, I'm done! I can't do this anymore! I can't take any more of this rejection. If I don't have an order by tomorrow, I'm quitting!"

God has such a sense of humor,

and yet He is sensitive to our call for help.

God has such a sense of humor, and yet He is sensitive to our call for help. The next morning, I walked into the office, and there, in the middle of my desk, was a purchase order. *Finally, an order,* I thought. When I looked at it, I was disappointed because it was only for $1,200. "Oh, man, that's hardly anything," I muttered.

What a terrible attitude! The first thing I did was start complaining.

Then God spoke to my heart, *Mani, you asked for an order. You didn't say how much.*

I laughed out loud. He was right, of course. I did ask for an order, and now I wouldn't quit. I guess, next time, I should set my sights higher.

By early November 2001, I had secured just eight sales in two years. I had visited potential clients across the United States and overseas, and had been told no by several hundred of them. We were at the very end of our funding to continue UNICAT. Even Jim's super positive and hopeful attitude toward the company was showing cracks; he began to doubt his investment, even though he tried to hide it, as I was pretty fragile by then. We had no idea that we were on the brink of a great adventure.

The Windows of Heaven

What happened in November and December 2001—in just two months—was beyond our wildest expectations! It could only be explained as the windows of heaven opening up and pouring down a blessing that could not be imagined.

Some manufacturing plants were willing to listen to our catalyst proposals, and so I prayed and visited them frequently. I was working on proposals for four major companies in 2001. I had captured their interest, and I was presenting our UNICAT products to them. I hoped we could secure at least one of the orders.

The largest prospect I was working with at the time was ConocoPhillips in Illinois. I met with their young and brilliant engineering staff for over eight months, learning their specific catalyst needs, answering their questions, and putting together proposals to help them improve their catalyst operations.

It was an exhilarating opportunity for us. We had learned that ConocoPhillips was planning to order replacement catalyst for all four units at their Syngas plant. I worked hard with their engineering staff, hoping and praying that we might receive the contract for just one of the units. We were a small company, with no successful history; one unit would be a great start for us.

Six weeks later, in early November, the fateful phone call came. Jim's office was directly across the hall from mine, so any time we received any business updates—which were usually bad—we could communicate immediately. We both were at our desks that morning when a phone call came that would change our lives.

"Mani," spoke a vaguely familiar voice over the phone, "this is the engineering department at ConocoPhillips. We wanted to let you know that we have made our decision. The team believes that you are the best candidate for this job. We have awarded UNICAT the full contract to replace the catalyst in all four of our catalyst units."

We had won the bid! I was stunned. Tears welled up in my eyes as I raced across the hall to Jim's office.

He had gotten up from his desk, and was walking toward the door because of all the commotion I was making.

"We got it, Jim! We got it!" I shouted.

He looked at me with a puzzled expression until I explained.

"Phillips has awarded us the contract! The entire contract—all four units! We're finally in business!"

I was so overjoyed that I laughed and cried. The order was five times bigger than my greatest expectations. Without a doubt, it was one of the best days in my life. The contract was worth one million dollars, and it was ours!

It was an unheard of situation! A major oil company was refitting their entire plant, four catalytic units, and they had just given the entire order to UNICAT, a brand-new company with no real success trail. It felt like a scene from a movie, only it was real!

We could hardly wait to get started. But, unfortunately, we had to wait a little longer than planned.

A week passed, then two weeks, but we still hadn't received the purchase order for the ConocoPhillips contract. I started to get a little nervous. I called their engineering department, and spoke with the young engineer who had been my greatest supporter. "What's going on?" I asked. "We haven't received your purchase order yet." As soon as he began to speak, my heart sank.

"I'm sorry, Mani, but the management team is reviewing the order again. This is very unusual, but they are questioning the engineering team's decision to hire you. They want to take a closer look at everything. I'm really sorry."

I started to get sick to my stomach. *Oh, no,* I thought, *this can't be happening again. A sure order gone sour.* I knew the management team always had the power to reverse the engineers' decisions, but I was praying that wasn't going to happen. The enemy was trying to rob us of God's blessings.

My heart was pounding in my chest when I asked him, "What can we do?"

"Mani, you have to come up here again and make another presentation. This time, it will be to the entire management team and all the engineers." Again. After eight months of proposals and work, and I needed to do it all again. *Well, I will just do it,* I thought. *I won't let the enemy walk all over me. I know that our product can help them. I know that we can complete this job. Help me, Lord.*

Jim and I flew to Illinois the next day. We knew that the chemical engineers at the plant were eager to work with us on this enormous project. It was the upper management that wanted answers to questions beyond what we had discussed with the engineers.

As I watched the management team file into the conference room that day, doubts crept into my mind. *There go our chances,* I thought. *Eight months of work with the engineering team down the tubes. There is no way this management team will award us—a small company with no experience—an entire plant. They would be risking their entire operation. Our chances are nil!* But then I reminded myself of God's promise in His Word "*What then shall we say to these things? If God is for us, who can be against us? He who did not spare His own Son, but delivered Him up for us all, how shall He not with Him also freely give us all things?"* (Romans 8:31–32 NKJV).

We Are the Perfect Choice

The management's questions began immediately: "How big is your company?" "How many employees do you have?" "Where will the catalyst be manufactured?" "What is your sales history?" "How will you meet our deadlines?"

We answered the questions honestly and without apology. Then I moved into my presentation, assuring them that our chemical catalyst would be the best choice to use in all four of their units. I reminded them that after months of spending time with their engineers, I understood their specific needs. UNICAT had developed innovative products that would give them successful results, our suppliers could handle their order in a timely manner, and our costs were lower than our competitors. "We are the perfect choice," I concluded.

When I finished, I sat down and thought, *Well, okay, we may have lost this order because we're new, but we presented the best choice for them today.*

As the meeting was ending, the young engineer stood up. (In our business, young chemical engineers do not stand up to management. They are trained to remain ultra-conservative in their decisions and are taught not to fix what's not broken.)

Then he said, "I want this order to go to UNICAT, as we originally promised them. I am willing to stake my job for it. No one else has helped me work with my units as they have in the last few months, and they have taught me things that no other vendor has to this day. I want to keep our original arrangement and grant them the contract."

With his words, the meeting was dismissed, and we all left. Jim and I just looked at each other, and knew what that young engineer had done was nothing short of a miracle. However, we also knew that the final decision lay in the Lord's hands. So we went home and waited.

One week later, the final word came—we had won the contract! God had moved in that young engineer's heart, and we had won the day! I will never forget that victory. It revealed the faithfulness of God and catapulted UNICAT and me toward the destiny God had called me to. It was the beginning of a new life.

God had moved in that young engineer's heart, and we had won the day! I will never forget that victory. It revealed the faithfulness of God and catapulted UNICAT and me toward the destiny God had called me to. It was the beginning of a new life.

Finally on the Move

A week later, I was at a hotel in Indonesia working on a catalyst proposal for a prospective customer when Jim called.

"Mani, you won't believe this! We just received a purchase order for BOC Group in Venezuela! It's another order, Mani! This one is for $250,000!"

"Glory to God" was my first response. We had actually received two orders in one month!

In early December, we received a third order, this time, from British Petroleum's manufacturing plant in Carson, California ($200,000). At that point, I got on my knees and cried like a baby.

"What are you doing here, Lord? Are you turning this whole thing around now?" I remembered Jim's words to me two years earlier, when God had told Jim that we needed to give Him two years. The Lord had work to do in the industry and in our hearts and lives. God's

Word was to be patient, persevere, and wait two years for the promise to be fulfilled.

The fourth order came from ATOFINA Petrochemicals, Inc., in Memphis, Tennessee ($100,000). The profits from those four business orders came into our offices exactly two years from the day Jim heard from the Lord. God is good!

These orders alone catapulted us into the big-time world of catalyst sales. We moved quickly from a nonplayer in the market to a viable, competitive business entity. It was an incredible success story, especially for a brand-new company, and it took the catalyst industry by surprise. Not only were we a real contender in the marketplace, we were also less expensive, more innovative, and had superior customer service. People in the oil industry sat up and took notice!

Realizing the Dream

My dream was coming to pass. Years of planning, months of working day and night, and days of presenting proposals were finally paying off. We had stepped into a new business realm, and our lives would never be the same. I can tell you that today, nearly seventeen years and many financial successes later, the thrill of those first four contracts still fills me with excitement! In early 2002, I was able to pay Jim back the half million dollars he had invested in UNICAT to get us up and running. We were on our way!

UNICAT's story is my life story. For more than eighteen years, it has been my professional life. It is the dream that I was "impregnated" with in my younger years, that I carried until I gave birth, and that I nurtured and protected so it could survive its perilous early years. UNICAT has grown steadily to become a very successful international catalyst company respected by the industry and competitors. Even now, with over $35 million in annual sales, UNICAT is experiencing a season of exponential growth, pushing it forward toward its ultimate destiny and purpose.

However, I must tell you that this victory didn't happen overnight. Believe me. It was a journey, and that journey is my real story.

Why did I choose to share this story with you? Because my story is not mine alone. I believe that my story can be a gateway to your success in the world of commerce. Every word I share, no matter how personal, is written in the hopes of being the kindling of a fire set alive in your own heart. Everyone has a story, and I know that you have one, too.

The Lessons I Needed to Learn

From the time that I graduated college, I always had a good job, and I always had a solid paycheck. I received raises and bonuses and promotions. I believed I was a person of faith. I honored God, I had faith for giving, I tithed, I paid my bills, I saved, I trusted God with my finances. This is what I always believed.

However, looking back, I can clearly see that what I really trusted was the only financial system I knew—the paycheck system. I had a paycheck that would arrive without fail twice every month. My trust was not really in Him; it was in the system.

In order to learn what it really means to trust the Lord, I had to stop depending on a paycheck. I had to die to the old system and the old way. I had to trust Him every month for my provision and pray that my bills would be paid. My old dependency had to die in my heart so that the new man—the man of faith—could be resurrected.

This could never have happened in just two months as I had hoped when we began. You know, the American way is instant success. It had to happen God's way. It had to be a process—His process. I walked the walk and used up all our savings and any safety nets I had from the old way until there were no resources left—only Him. Quite honestly, it got really scary.

During that time, multiple people questioned me, "Mani, what are you doing?" and "Why are you doing this?"

Another said, "I have this great job offer for you, Mani; it's a $100,000 salary. Come work for me."

> *God wanted me to do something that required me to trust Him, something that proved success had nothing to do with me. I had to totally fail so that my success would always be in Him.*

However, God wanted me to do something that required me to trust Him, something that proved success had nothing to do with me. I had to totally fail so that my success would always be in Him. I was called to be His disciple to the world. In place of bonuses and raises were failures. He trained me to be His man with hundreds of them. I reached a place where I had lost my self-confidence, which I had always counted on in the sales world. Remember, I was the man who could travel the world for forty-two weeks and build a flourishing business success out of nothing. Not anymore. Now God would mold me into the image of His success and not my own. I had to reach a place where there was no way I could succeed. It had to be God.

God stripped me clean—I was naked before Him. I felt totally hopeless, completely dependent on His grace. And over and over, He provided for me and my family. I don't even know how.

Learning to Really Trust

It is hard to explain the closeness I had with the Lord during those two difficult years. When you are relying on Him for everything, you develop a special bond with Him. I experienced His presence, peace, and reassurance.

I have to confess that these were some of the happiest years of my life. The communion I had with the Lord was that amazing. It was the hardest time, but it was the happiest time. I sensed the Lord's presence with me so often. He reassured me and gave me the strength to get up each day and try again. Those two years made me into a real man of faith in my finances.

Now I understand why the Lord took me down that road. I realize how important it was to survive, thrive, and make it through the valley. During that time, God tested my faith and my character. He allowed me to die to my own understanding, and awaken to His ways and His purposes for my life.

I honestly believe it was a trust issue all the way around. He was building my trust and seeing if He could trust me. Could God trust me with the millions of dollars that would come in through the success of UNICAT? Could He trust me to use a sizeable portion of that money to build His kingdom and not to spend it on myself? Would it corrupt me, or would I use it for His glory? Perhaps the man I once was couldn't be trusted, but the man He created me to be through those two long years could be trusted.

I would not trade those two years for anything in the world. They made me the businessman and the man of God I am today. That is why I am so emphatic about the importance of embracing our difficulties. Those years were a gift from God. At the time, I called them a struggle, but truly they were a gift!

I want to give God all the recognition and honor that belongs to Him for the success that UNICAT had then and all the years after. If I had any role in that success at all, it was that I remained steadfast during those lean and difficult early years. I held ground and, at times, I fell down, but God was there to pick me up. I cried and felt hopeless at times, I was disappointed many times, and I was rewarded only a few times, but I did not quit!

That is all I can say to anyone who is going through tribulation and testing. I know how you feel. I have been there. Everyone's story is different, but in the end, we all have the choice to quit or to keep on running the race in pursuit of our destiny.

Is your destiny and future worth fighting for? Then stand, don't quit, and don't despise the days of small beginnings; they may be some of the best days of your life.

7

HE HAS YOUR BACK

If I wanted to share all the stories of God intervening and saving UNICAT through extraordinary miracles, I would have to write a separate book. Time and time again, we have been saved from financial ruin and serious consequences, and the only thing we could attribute our great escape to was God's divine intervention on our behalf. Heavenly miracles have surrounded UNICAT from the day its doors were opened.

I would like to share a few of these stories with you. My desire is that sharing with you will glorify the Father and bring hope to any Christian who is setting sail on his or her destiny. God has our back, and He is faithful to complete what He started in us.

> *He who has begun a good work in you will complete it until the day of Jesus Christ.* (Philippians 1:6 NKJV)

The Iowa Carbon Miracle

In early 2001, we received an order (one of the eight I landed during those first two meager years) from a company in Iowa for a carbon-based product. We would have sent that order to our plant in China, but the product was simple enough, and Jim had a friend in Houston that assured us he could make it, so we went with a locally made catalyst.

I should have known better than to change our supplier so early in the game. The product was produced on time, but I should have suspected a problem, because the Houston manufacturer had asked me several times about production details they should have already known.

On the day of commissioning, when the buyer launches the new product in his plant, I got a phone call that no manufacturers ever want to receive from the plant manager.

"What is this yellow-and-blue smoke coming out of my vent stack? What kind of product have you sold me?"

It turned out that the color coming out of the stack was the active chemical used to make the carbon product. My heart sank when I realized that the US manufacturer had failed to fix the chemical onto the carbon by proper treatment, and now it was leaving the system through a vent stack. It was an operational and, potentially, environmental disaster.

The plant manager was crystal clear. The unit was shut down immediately to prevent any more of the colored effluent from escaping out of the stack. He insisted that I replace the product immediately, and take full liability for any environmental damages or fines issued from any government agency.

My first reaction was to panic! Although this was disheartening, we had a much bigger problem. If news of this failure spread all over the industry, UNICAT would be finished; our reputation would be severely damaged early in the company's history.

I walked into Jim's office with the weight of the world on my shoulders.

He heard me out and then said, "Let's pray."

We both knelt down and started to pray on the floor of our small office in Alvin, Texas.

After a few minutes, Jim spoke confidently, "Don't worry about it, Mani. I believe that God just told me He took care of it. Just tell them to start up the unit one more time, and it will work fine."

What? You have to be kidding me! Tell them to start up the unit again? I looked Jim in the eyes. "Jim," I said raggedly, "don't you understand that once they start the operation up again, if there is color spewing out of the stack, we will be environmentally liable!"

I admit I was afraid. The cost of replacing the catalyst product was forty thousand dollars, which was a lot of money for us at that time; plus, I did not trust the guy in Houston. Now, I would have to go find it from someone else, but no other manufacturer had it on hand at the time. My whole body was shaking as I considered the extent of the disaster. Surely, this would be the day my dream of UNICAT's success would come to an abrupt and ugly end!

Jim's confidence was not one bit shaken by my anxiety. He spoke what the Lord had told him with certainty, as if it was a done deal and the issue had already been resolved. Trembling, I walked out on that branch of faith with him. I picked up the phone, called the plant manager, and told him to start up the unit one more time. He repeated his position again—if any off-color gas escaped from that vent, he would unload the product immediately, analyze the vent gas, and report it to the Environmental Protection Agency, as the law required. We would be financially responsible for the cleanup, the replacement product, and all fines.

> *I reminded myself that God had called me to start this business, and that God would not let it end like this.*

My heart sank. What could I say or do? I started praying again. I reminded myself that God had called me to start this business, and that God would not let it end like this. But, at the same time, I kept chiding myself for switching our production to another company when we had the opportunity to order from a dependable supplier in China. This fiasco was caused by my poor decision.

The moment of truth came. The customer planned to start the unit the next morning, so I came in early and sat by the phone expecting the call—but the call never came. By late afternoon, I couldn't wait any longer; I called the plant and asked the engineers if they had restarted the unit. The answer was a miracle. Yes, they had restarted that morning, right on schedule, and no off-color gas was observed. Whew! That was such a relief! Now I was curious, why had there ever been off-colored gas, and what made it stop? Perhaps all the chemical ingredients needed on the carbon had been dislodged in the previous start-up. If that had happened, I would be getting another angry call in a few weeks; the unit would never make it through its targeted ninety-day cycle, and the customer would demand product replacement! Our reputation was still on the line.

I bet you can guess where I'm going with this. The unit not only made it past the ninety days, it actually produced for more than one hundred ten days. The customer was happy. We were happy. We were not penalized at all, and the problem was resolved! I knew there was a miracle here, because the active ingredients were stripped off, and the catalyst should not have lasted even half that time. I can almost imagine God's angels asking for clarification on instructions they had received on how to put the active chemicals back on the catalyst!

The company was saved, once again, and all I could remember were Jim's words: "Mani, God has just taken care of it."

Wow, what a God we serve!

The Miracle of Supply for Saudi Arabia

By January 2003, things at UNICAT were going well. We were gaining new customers at a steady rate. Just a month before, I had sold a large order to an oil refinery in Saudi Arabia. The order was another miracle of sorts, since it seemed impossible that we could land an order from a large overseas refinery so early in our company. The customer was extremely timid about choosing us at first. They needed the product at their plant within nine weeks from the date of order.

In our line of work, a critical delivery time is vital in fulfilling an order. Four weeks had passed, and we were ready to ship the product from one of our Chinese suppliers to Saudi Arabia.

Then came a phone call from the sales manager of our direct competitor. Why was he calling me? After a few minutes of casual conversation, he asked me if I was looking for a job.

I was surprised by the question and responded, "Of course not. I have my own company, and I am happy doing what I am doing."

He chuckled and replied, "Well, you will be looking for a job soon, so I just wanted to let you know I am looking for a few good people, and I would like to hire you."

Bewildered, I hung up the phone. What had happened that this man thought I would be out of business soon?

The next day, the bad news came. Without any warning, our direct competitor purchased the main Chinese plant that we had contracted to supply most of our catalyst products. The new company had instructed the plant not to sell any products to us now or in the future, cancel any current sales contracts with us, and not to ship any products that had already been made for us!

Knowing how dog-eat-dog our industry was, we had started preparing ourselves for something like this by diversifying our supply chain and connecting with a number of other suppliers. But his was still bad news on top of bad news and, believe it or not, it got even worse. Another phone call came from our agent in Saudi Arabia. Our direct competitor had informed them of the purchase of the plant in China, and had warned them of our inability to supply. The customer was very concerned. The Saudis wanted to know if the rumors were true. Since they needed the product in five weeks, and the competitor had it in stock (no surprise, since it was our product!), they wanted to place the order with them and cancel ours.

What a fiasco! How could we ever solve this one? If I were to accept the cancellation, then the whole oil industry would know we were not able to meet our obligations. No one would trust us to supply them with products in the future, and certainly we would lose face with our Saudi customer.

> *I knew that trusting God was our only hope for an answer. On our knees, we prayed for divine protection and a miracle.*

They needed an answer right away, but I had no solution for them. I asked my agent to give me one more day to work it out. Then I called my Chinese partner, Eric Lui, and asked him what we could possibly do to save the order. He told me that he had tried to force the plant to honor their original order with us but to no avail. He knew of only one other plant in China that could manufacture the same product, but they had no stock on hand, so it would take eight weeks before they could make it.

Jim and I started praying. The Bible says, "*The effective prayer of a righteous man can accomplish much*" (James 5:16 NASB). I knew that trusting God was our only hope for an answer. On our knees, we prayed for divine protection and a miracle. A few hours later, in the middle of the night, I got a call from Eric. He had flown to the second plant in China and found out that they had a load of catalyst that was the exact same type and quantity we needed already stored in their warehouse for another customer. Eric believed that our only hope was to convince that customer to sell this catalyst to us, and then have them wait eight weeks until we could replace their order.

I was cautiously optimistic. Here was a possible answer when, a few hours earlier, I had not been able to see any way to get out of this mess. Eric wasn't sure if we could swing the switch with the Chinese customer whose goods were now in storage, but it was late afternoon in Saudi Arabia, and I had to make a decision. I decided to be bold and act on faith. I told the Saudi agent not to worry, that their product would be delivered in five weeks, as promised. Whew! God had shown me that He had a plan, and I had to trust Him in it.

I made the call, and we were fully committed again. No way out! We needed the other customer in China to let us use their product. Three days passed with no news. I'm sure I lost a few pounds thinking about it almost every minute of the day. The constant phone calls from Saudi Arabia didn't help, either, the caller seeking confirmation over and over again that we really could deliver and reminding us of the consequences of not making good on our promises.

Finally, incredible news came. Eric had secured the cargo! He had moved it to port quickly, the goods were safely on their way to Saudi Arabia, and would make it with time to spare! Eric had slept in his car for several days while visiting the end user in China, pleading with them to let us purchase their goods. He secured the agreement and worked nonstop to move the cargo to port, labeling it and loading it on an early ship.

I can't imagine what he had to go through, but I also know that God's hand was at work in all this. Eric's diligence and God's divine favor working together, plus an act of faith on our part, not giving in to fear, led to one of the greatest miracles in our company's history.

Our competitor was embarrassed in front of the Saudi customer, since all their accusations about our inability to deliver were proven false. Because of my background in the Middle East, we also were able to provide excellent service to the Saudi customer while facing some very difficult international circumstances. You see, their catalyst unit startup was scheduled for March 2003, the same month the United States and the Multinational Force–Iraq (also called the coalition forces) launched Operation Iraqi Freedom. While every contractor was fleeing Saudi Arabia in fear, I flew in and remained seven days to do my job. I stayed in a nearly empty hotel, and the Saudi oil company was highly appreciative that we could see the job through in spite of the circumstances. This was a radical turn of events for UNICAT in the Middle East and led to many subsequent orders.

A few weeks later, I received another call from our competitor; it was the same manager who had called me earlier to tell me that I would soon be out of business. He was dumbfounded; how did we manage to find the supply? Then, in a great twist of irony, he asked me if I could still use the material that was left in his warehouse! It was hard not to laugh, it was so ironic. The overstock was as a result of their greed, and the Lord protected us from it all.

Many companies have tried to eliminate us over the years by approaching our suppliers and trying to dismantle our supply chain. But after seventeen years, we are still here, and we are stronger than ever. God always has had our back, and He proved to me once again that this was far bigger than me or Jim or a business venture that produced some money. It was about lifting up His name and fulfilling His promises and His purposes for UNICAT.

He is not going to let us fail.

We can never repay the Lord for what He has done for us. At times, God has used men to bless us and supply the miracle, and, other times, He unilaterally moved on our behalf. Jim has seen countless miracles of favor and protection in his work in China, and I have seen countless miracles of protection everywhere else.

One thing is certain—if we trust in God and obey Him, the burden of protection and blessings falls on Him and not on us. What a relief! We no longer have to have every answer and the solution to every problem.

We who call God by name and have decided to obey and enter into our destiny walk and live in His grace and remain under the shadow of the Almighty.

> *He who dwells in the secret place of the Most High shall abide under the shadow of the Almighty. I will say of the* Lord, *"He is my refuge and my fortress; my God, in Him I will trust."*
>
> (Psalm 91:1–2)

So rest in Him, my friends, because He has got your back!

8

CRAZY IDEAS CAN SUCCEED

I often wonder if God gets tremendous pleasure out of amazing us by defying human logic. In God's kingdom, any idea or thought that emanates from His throne cannot find a common thread within our human logic. If it did, we—with our inherent God-complexes—would consider them as our own creative ideas and eventually take full credit for our own success. But, as Christians know well, God shares His glory with no one.

It must be fun for the Lord to come up with some of the unbelievable circumstances that must play out in perfect sequence for His miracles to become reality in our lives. Of course, we have to cooperate with Him for it to all work out. But I can say with utmost confidence that man cannot find one ounce of human logic or "this makes good sense" in heaven's methodology.

An Incredibly Crazy Idea

In the middle of all the hard work launching UNICAT, I had not forgotten about my call to share the gospel with the Muslims in the Middle East, particularly Iran. During this time, I heard a promise from God that would take first prize in the "incredibly crazy idea" category. God spoke to my heart about who would fund my ministry to Iranian Muslims.

Years before I launched UNICAT, I had been involved in sharing the gospel with Muslims in and around the city of Houston. For me, it was a foregone conclusion that, one day, I would take the gospel far beyond the borders of Houston and the United States, sharing God's salvation with Muslims around the globe. That much of my future ministry God had already revealed to me. Although I was not sure how this was going to come to pass, I knew in my heart that the businesses I would start would fund this ministry.

One day, I would take the gospel far beyond the borders of the United States, sharing God's salvation with Muslims around the globe. That much of my future ministry God had already revealed to me. Although I was not sure how this was going to come to pass, I knew in my heart that the businesses I would start would fund this ministry.

Then, while I was still working hard to start up UNICAT, God told me something that absolutely floored me. I believe He spoke because He wanted me to recognize that everything that would happen to me in the next few years was not my own doing but His divine hand in action. It was His way of declaring that He was in charge of it all, from start to finish.

The promise went something like this: "Muslims from Saudi Arabia and the Middle East will pay for most of your ministry expenses one day!" And, just what was my ministry goal? Preaching the gospel of Jesus Christ to those very same Muslims!

What? Of all the crazy and ridiculous things I could have heard, this was at the top of the list. If I would ever share it with anyone, they would think I had lost my mind. I couldn't begin to imagine how Muslims from the most restrictive regions of the Islamic world would ever support the work of the ministry I was going to do. In Islam, converting Muslims to a living faith in Jesus Christ is the worst possible offense. Why would any Muslim pay me to preach the gospel to another Muslim?

How Commerce Can Pay for Ministry

Of course, Muslims did not directly pay for my future Christian ministries, but the commerce that I contracted with them would pay for many outreaches in years to come. Let me explain. Shortly after we launched UNICAT, I started a consulting business on the side to help provide for my family. The money I have made the last sixteen years through my second business, IRA Consulting, comes directly from my work with Muslim business leaders in the Middle East.

IRA Consulting is a metal-trading business related to the work that I had done in the waste recycling business. In fact, in my seven years working in industrial recycling, I had learned about an entirely new industry that was going to be used by God to pour finances into my life and into His work.

In 1995, while on a business trip for the recycling company, I traveled to Saudi Arabia for the very first time. What an eye-opening initial visit. First, the eight-minute flight from Bahrain to Saudi Arabia took two hours because of a drunk British passenger whom the crew was trying to sober up before landing. Then, I spent five hours going through customs in the King Fahd International Airport in Dammam, Saudi Arabia, while custom agents went through literally every piece of my luggage, listening to each and every tape (worship and sermons) I had brought with me for personal use before confiscating them all.

I remember finally getting out of the airport, breathing in the Saudi air, and feeling an incredible heaviness, as if a ton of weight had been placed on my shoulders. I could feel the spiritual darkness, and I sensed that my spirit was being pressured from all sides. This was, after all, the birthplace of Islam and home to the two holy mosques of Mecca and Medina. Saudi Arabia is the very epicenter of the kingdom of Islam, and all the spiritual forces that govern it. How God would turn the hearts of men living in such a country to support the work of His ministry was beyond my comprehension.

During my first trip, I met two Muslim gentlemen, one from Kuwait and the other from Saudi Arabia. These businessmen eventually became two of my very best friends and, in the course of the next four years, I conducted numerous projects with them on behalf of my employer. Once I left the company and began the work with UNICAT, I called both these Middle Eastern businessmen, and asked if they were open to participating in a metal-trading business with me. Their enthusiastic response was more than I ever expected!

Let me explain just how big a miracle their positive responses were. In the metal-trading business, you need two things to be successful: first, the ability to finance your operations so that you can purchase goods in advance and then survive for three to four months while waiting for your money to come back; second, good business connections established with buyers and sellers, and the infrastructure to protect the identity of your buyers from your sellers. Obviously, if these two business partners got to know each another, my position as a middleman trader would no longer be necessary.

I did not have any finances to speak of at the time, but I did have very good connections with the buyers, and I knew my sellers in the Middle East. When working for the waste recycling company, we protected our buyers from the people in Saudi Arabia and Kuwait so that they didn't know exactly where we were shipping the traded goods. But now, working for myself, I had no choice but to let the buyers and sellers know each other, and trust that they would not go around me. "Lord," I prayed, "what steps should I take to make this work out?"

With the encouragement of the Lord to move forward, I contacted both men, and proposed what would have seemed like a ridiculous business proposition. I told them that I was about to start my own venture in the metal-trading business. Then I admitted that I did not have the capital to initially pay for the goods but that I would have to wait for the payment from the buyer before I could pay them. This was an absolute no-no in our business, and I knew it. I asked them to operate like this for one or two years until I could accumulate the necessary financial reserves.

Next, I told them the most preposterous part of my plan—I would let them know who my buyers were because I did not have the logistics to protect the parties from knowing one another. I knew that I would have to trust them never to knock me out as the middleman to keep the extra profit margin for themselves. Let me put it this way: my friends in the Middle East knew that I was making money by receiving their goods and selling them to companies they could identify. And yet, in all these years, they have never tried to go around me to keep the extra profit. Honestly, this makes no sense at all when you think about the world of trading!

How can I even explain the Lord's faithfulness in what happened next? Both of those businessmen willingly gave up significant amounts of money by doing business with me, and they did so without asking me to pay them in advance!

This, my friend, is called favor in the kingdom of God.

Over the years, both men have sent millions of dollars in business my way when they could have, with one simple phone call, made an additional 20–40 percent by sending their metal goods directly to my buyers. So, even though these men were Muslims, and knew that I was a Christian who had converted from Islam, they allowed me to make hundreds of thousands of dollars in additional profit from our business arrangement.

I told them that I was born and raised as a Muslim and that I had converted to Christianity. Frankly, on that basis alone, they should have rejected doing any business with me, let alone become my friends. Not only did they not reject me, they blessed me and continue to do so to this very day. Now that is what I call favor and a kingdom miracle!

Yes, you read it right. Early in our relationship, I told them that I was born and raised as a Muslim and that I had converted to Christianity. Frankly, on that basis alone, they should have rejected doing any business with me, let alone become my friends. Not only did they not reject me, they blessed me and continue to do so to this very day.

Now that is what I call favor and a kingdom miracle!

I often have asked them why they blessed me, and their response has been something like this: "We like you, Mani. We trust you, and we feel comfortable doing business with you."

It is as though they are saying, "Even though it isn't logical, it has been placed in our hearts to have great favor toward you."

We see this same story played out in the Bible numerous times. Men of God often found refuge and help from men or rulers of foreign lands who did not acknowledge Him. Abraham found refuge in Egypt. Joseph found great favor in Pharaoh's eyes. Isaac and David both found safety with the Philistines and their rulers. Ezra and Nehemiah found favor with the Persian kings and received the wealth they needed to rebuild God's house in Jerusalem. Who can ever forget Esther and her favor-filled life story? Joseph and Mary fled to Egypt to protect God's Son Jesus, and the examples go on.

Now, years later, I can say with absolute confidence that I have made millions of dollars through IRA Consulting, invested in Christian ministry and the spread of the gospel all over the world, and this work has been directly sourced from transactions with these Muslim men living in the heart of the kingdom of Islam.

The Lord is a loving God of the miraculous and the amazing. He has His hand on our destiny.

9

THE PURPOSE BEHIND THE PROMISE

Our God is a master planner, and He never does anything without a divine and perfect purpose behind it. When He created us, He had a purpose set aside for each and every one of us, and a destiny planned that we were uniquely designed to accomplish. We are never complete outside of this divine purpose; we find our highest level of fulfillment and joy when we are pursuing it.

Finding your kingdom assignment is the most important thing you can do in your lifetime. As Christians, we all have an identity as children of the King. Kings are conqueror dreamers. Those with a personal destiny in business have to be dreamers and conquerors;

they certainly can't be timid or afraid! They have to have a bold spirit. However, as a Christian, just being bold and crazy or willing to take risks for God is not enough to succeed if you don't know the ultimate reason behind it. There is not enough motivation to fight through the enormous challenges that come against us—especially for Christian business owners. We need to know why we are doing what we are doing because making money just to make money is not a good enough reason for a kingdom-minded Christian.

Finding our purpose—our kingdom assignment—is critical to the overall success of our Christian-owned and -operated business.

Finding our purpose—our kingdom assignment—is critical to the overall success of our Christian-owned and -operated business.

I had a clear idea in my second year of business that UNICAT and IRA Consulting were to be used to fund the spread of the gospel of Jesus Christ to the nation of Iran and the greater Muslim world through media and satellite television. This was going to take money, and, somehow, UNICAT and IRA Consulting were going to supply it.

My Call to Ministry

In 1996, four years before my businesses launched, I began to pastor a small Iranian Christian church in Houston, Texas. The church was small, with around eighty members, and financially was only able to cover its basic needs. Then, in June 2000, during prayer, God laid a vision on my heart. He was calling me to develop a television ministry to reach the lost people of Iran. Whoa, how would I do this? At first, it seemed like just another wild idea. UNICAT had just launched, and I was in over my head.

It was a very challenging and difficult period, not only because the church and my personal finances could not begin to set up this ministry, but because no technology was in place for anyone to broadcast the gospel of Jesus Christ in Iran at that time. No television stations or broadcasting companies were dedicated to sending a television signal into the heart of the Middle East. And to reach people in Iran, the broadcast would have to be in Farsi, the Iranian native language. Anyway, who in the world would want to watch Christian television in the Islamic Republic of Iran? After all, Iran was the very epicenter of Islamic revolutionary zealotry.

Naturally, as God would have it, that was exactly what He had in mind! I chewed on the idea during the summer and early fall of 2000 with no sign that it could come to pass. The business was still struggling, I had no money to purchase any broadcasting equipment or rent a studio, the church was as poor as ever, and Iran was still Iran, with no visible change.

Then, in November 2000, I got a call from an Iranian friend. Afshin was a young man who had attended our church in Houston a few years earlier and was now living in Midland, Texas, working on an oil-drilling site. He called to talk about a local Christian television station called God's Learning Channel, broadcasting out of Odessa. After hearing about our Iranian ministry, the Christian owners wanted to interview me on live television. I was immediately intrigued. I had never been on television before; maybe this was a sign from heaven. So I took the opportunity, paid for a ticket out of my limited finances, hopped on a plane, and flew to Midland.

As soon as I walked off the plane, I was convinced that there was no way anything in Odessa or Midland could remotely connect with Iran or a Muslim outreach. This west Texas, oil-patch town probably didn't have even a handful of Iranians in it. Once again, my own eagerness to see God's visions come to pass had gotten the best of me.

Coming to Odessa was simply a mistake, and a waste of my very limited time and resources.

Once I arrived at the station, the feeling intensified. This was not a normal Trinity Broadcasting Network (TBN) television station. In fact, with Jewish banners and artifacts displayed all over the set, it looked more like a Jewish television station than an evangelical Christian one. The owners, Tommie and Al Cooper, welcomed me warmly, and we sat down to start the interview. My first television experience went by without anything spectacular happening. We talked about God and Christian ministry, and then I was on a plane headed back to Houston. Even though it went without a hitch, I was 100 percent convinced I had missed the Lord's guidance by going to Midland. Before landing in Houston, I told myself that I would not go back, even if invited. When will I learn not to say "no," or "never," until I have prayed and heard from God?

Several months later, I got a call from the station manager, asking me to please come back to Midland for a second interview! I was about to politely decline when the Holy Spirit prompted me to say yes. I started arguing with Him in my head, but it was clear in my heart that I was supposed to go. After hanging up the phone, I asked the Lord, "Why do you want me to go back? There is nothing there for me or the ministry."

His reply was clear enough: "I need you to go back and give the owners a message from Me. It needs to be in person, and you need to do it on live television."

"What kind of message, Lord?"

"You need to warn them that they have forgotten about Samaria and the remote parts of the world. They are preaching only to Jerusalem and Judea, and I have blessed them to reach the nations with their television station—the Jews and beyond. If they don't change their course, they will lose the blessing."

"You want me to do what on live television? Lord, this is too much to ask of me. They don't even know me. I can't just go there and tell them this on my second visit and on live television!"

Well, as you can imagine, I got nothing back from the Lord except, "You know what you have to do, so get down and do it!"

"Sorry, I Can't Sign It"

With the date and time set for the interview, I found myself in Midland a second time. However, on this trip, my nerves were on edge, and I paced back and forth in the station's green room. While I waited to go on, the program director walked in, handed me a piece of paper, and asked me to sign it. When I asked what it was, he said that it was a formality that all guests had to sign, an agreement to follow a certain code of conduct, including a promise not to ever correct or admonish the host on live television!

"Well," I said firmly, "I'm afraid I can't sign it."

The director looked shocked and spoke hastily, "You are going on the air in five minutes, and I can't let you go on unless you sign this paper!"

"Sorry, I can't sign it."

While he left to determine what to do with me, an assistant came and whisked me away to the interview area. I sat in front of the camera just one minute before airtime and could see the program director having a quiet discussion with several of the staff. It was obvious that they had resigned themselves to allowing me to go on air without signing the agreement.

The interview started without any issues, but as the clock started winding down to the end of the program, I could hear the Holy Spirit saying to me, "It's time to make your statement and warn the Coopers." Twenty minutes left, and my heart started racing. Ten minutes, and my heart was pounding faster than ever. I could feel the pressure building up within me, and I was truly scared. Five minutes before the end of the program, and the Holy Spirit shouted vehemently in my heart, "Do what I told you to do right now!" Finally, mustering every bit of courage I could, I turned to Al Cooper, and told him I had a message for him from the Lord. He smiled, and I started speaking, "Al, you know that the Word says, '*But you will receive power when the Holy Spirit comes on you; and you will be my witnesses in Jerusalem, and in all Judea and Samaria, and to the ends of the earth*'" (Acts 1:8). Then I explained to him that God wanted him to take the gift of that television station and bless many nations—not just one or two; otherwise, the blessings would not remain.

In the twinkling of an eye, God opened the doors for me to reach Iran with the gospel though media. I had access to more equipment, people, and resources than I could have ever dreamed possible, and all of it at no cost to the ministry or me.

I vividly remember the next few seconds because they seemed to go on for an eternity! Al simply looked at me. There was absolute quiet on the set, and on a live television program, the silence was deafening. I had no idea what he was going to do or say, but I prepared myself for a quick exit and a run back to my car to leave Midland and never come back.

After about thirty seconds of silence, he simply asked, "Mani, didn't you tell me that God has called you to reach Iran with television and satellite ministry?"

"Yes, for sure."

"Then, Mani, consider this television station with all of its equipment and staff as part of your ministry to reach Iran. You can tape here for free, and we will broadcast your programs for free. Consider it our investment in your mission to Iran."

I could not believe my ears! Tears welled up in my eyes. In the twinkling of an eye, God opened the doors for me to reach Iran with the gospel though media. I had access to more equipment, people, and resources than I could have ever dreamed possible, and all of it at no cost to the ministry or me.

As it turned out, this was the very beginning of our television ministry. I ended up flying to Midland several times that year, and I produced twelve thirty-minute programs in Farsi for Iranian Muslims. I had no idea how or when they would be broadcast directly to Iran, but I had all the resources to produce them in the most professional manner, and all this in Midland, Texas. This was the beginning of my God-given assignment, and it was initiated at the same time UNICAT was launched. I had been placed squarely in God's perfect will for my life.

When our programs started airing, they were the first Christian television programs ever to be broadcast in the nation of Iran. More than one million people were reached in the first broadcast alone.

Almost ten months later, just after the attack on the World Trade Center in September 2001, the very first Farsi satellite television station was born. As Pars TV looked desperately for Farsi-based programs to broadcast to the Iranian people (back in those days, they didn't care if it was Christian-themed or not; they just wanted content), guess who was ready and waiting with twelve professionally filmed Christian segments ready to broadcast? God's goodness and perfect timing overwhelm me even when I think of it today.

When our programs started airing, they were the first Christian television programs ever to be broadcast in the nation of Iran. More than one million people were reached in the first broadcast alone. This was the beginning of my worldwide ministry, which we named Christ for the Crescent Moon (CCM) Evangelical Ministries. UNICAT and IRA Consulting have been financially supporting it ever since.

The Point of It All

Brothers and sisters, this is the point of it all—all the work in building a business and launching a ministry. It is to see lives changed for eternity with the message of salvation through Jesus Christ. Years have passed since my first television broadcast, and thousands of Muslim souls have been touched and changed through the gospel of our Lord Jesus Christ. During those years, UNICAT's very existence and why I had been uniquely chosen to start the company became crystal clear to me. I had a call on my life to reach Muslims, particularly Iranians, for the sake of the gospel, and I was gifted as a businessman and salesman. God combined every asset and calling He had placed within me for the completion of my unique purpose and destiny.

He has a vision and purpose set aside for everyone today. It is our job to obey and release ourselves into His hands and His job to fulfill the destiny He has imbedded into our born-again spirits.

I believe God's desire is that we discover that destiny and find a pathway to success in it. I also believe that many Christians are called to the world of commerce, to be successful there, and to use their success to expand God's kingdom. In the following pages, I want to share the critical keys to success I have discovered along the way, as God has unfolded His true purpose for my life. Continue this journey with me.

PART 2:
CRITICAL KEYS TO REACH SUCCESS

10

APPRENTICESHIP: LEARNING FROM THE BEST

Powerful principles for success have played a huge role in reaching a destiny beyond my hopes and dreams. In the next few chapters, I want to share them since they have been my constant companions on the journey. They include apprenticeship; multiplication and duplication; timing, risk, and failure; and the dominion mandate and the principle of wealth transfer. God used them to bring me to the victory I am experiencing in business and ministry today. I have written this book because I passionately believe these key insights will help you successfully fulfill your own destiny.

The first principle is a practical necessity in the business world, and we don't see it nearly enough today—the art of apprenticeship.

I have one question to ask all you college-educated folks out there who have invested many years in libraries studying, tens of thousands of dollars for tuition, and a good chunk of your youth in the classrooms of modern universities: was it worth the investment?

Of course, the answer depends entirely on the type of professional endeavor you have chosen for yourself. It all depends on the road you are taking.

Personally, I find it amazing that in some fields of study, the art of apprenticeship is practiced as a mandate, but in many other fields, it is completely forgotten. After medical school, doctors must spend four years working as residents before earning their stripes, laboring away in hospitals for next to nothing, doing all the dirty work other doctors are not willing to do. Residencies have been required in the medical field for as long as anyone can remember. No one wants to throw a young medical doctor out there treating patients if he or she has not put into actual practice all the medical theories learned, and no one is better equipped to teach them than a physician who has successfully practiced medicine for years.

This applies to the field of teaching, as well. Young teachers-in-training must spend at least a semester student teaching to learn the ropes under the guidance of an experienced teacher.

So my question is, why doesn't it apply to the field of commerce and business? Young people used to be required to complete an apprenticeship before entering business. But today, no one requires new employees or college graduates to invest two to four years of their life learning the ins and outs of business under the watchful eye of truly successful business people.

Each year, universities turn out thousands of students with business and marketing degrees who, frankly, have no clue how to run a real business. I remember what happened to the metal-recycling business where I was employed. The owner had run it successfully for twenty-six years, making a huge annual profit. After I left, he turned the day-to-day operations of the company over to a Harvard-educated businessman, who had multiple degrees in business and finance but little experience in making money the old-fashioned way. That man managed to run the business into the ground and into bankruptcy within four short years.

In the Bible, we see the principle of teacher and apprentice over and over again. In 1 and 2 Kings, the prophet Elijah takes Elisha under his wing for fourteen years, training the next great prophet of Israel. Before long, the student outshone his teacher in the history of the Jewish nation.

In several letters of the New Testament, Paul takes Timothy under his wing to produce a strong disciple of Christ. Finally, the greatest teacher of all, Jesus Christ, took the twelve disciples through three and a half years of field training, losing only one pupil to the wiles of the devil. Look what the other eleven were able to accomplish as they spread the gospel of Jesus Christ throughout the known world in their lifetimes.

Apprenticeship Is Key to Extraordinary Success

I am convinced that the art of apprenticeship is desperately needed in the field of commerce. Beyond that, I am convinced it is a major key to success. Read this carefully: If you wish to succeed in business, you need to invest your time and energy in learning business skills at the most practical level, working for a business leader or an organization that has already been down the road of success, emulating the traits and skills that have made them successful. There are multiple ways to accomplish this, but in my opinion, an internship—learning from someone already skilled—is a mandatory and obligatory part of anyone's path to success.

Of course, young bright entrepreneurs have built multibillion dollar businesses with no prior business experience or while still in college. Bill Gates of Microsoft and Mark Zuckerberg of Facebook come to mind. But they are exceptions, not the norm. I can certainly attest from experience that apprenticeship, and the way God led me to use it in my life, was one of the main keys to my extraordinary success.

> *If you wish to succeed in business,*
> *you need to invest your time and energy in learning business skills at the most practical level, working for a business leader or an organization that has already been down the road of success, emulating the traits and skills that have made them successful.*

In my case, the successful track of UNICAT and IRA Consulting is the direct result of the skills I acquired while working as an employee at other companies. The ten years I invested in those companies were not wasted. Remember, it was not just me going to a job and coming home with a nice paycheck. I made an intentional decision to work hard and learn the skills of the trade, the ins and outs of successful commerce, the dos and don'ts for my own future venture. I watched the way successful people in my field handled adversity and took careful note of what they did, both right and wrong. These lessons were vividly recorded in my memory.

I apprenticed for ten years while earning a fraction of what I could have earned had I been in my own business. But it was a far better investment in my future than any other I could have made. Medical interns make a fraction of what they will earn once they are board-certified physicians. We should consider the years of field training as an investment in ourselves and in our future.

Too many people end up jumping into businesses that they have no experience in, and then must learn the ropes the hard way, mistake after mistake. Sometimes, by the time they learn what they need to learn, the business is no longer viable. They either run out of cash or time or both. Others jump from one job to another simply trying to earn a raise or make a higher salary, but they never stay long enough to learn the traits they need to make an actual business work for them.

My suggestion is to choose what business you believe you are called to, then trust that direction and set your eyes on it. Next, develop a strategic plan to enter that specific business environment or a similar one through employment. During your time there, observe, ask questions, and learn all you can while working hard to be the best employee you can be. It is our duty and responsibility to give our best to those who have entrusted us with our jobs, but there is no reason why we cannot earn our "real" business degree at the same time.

If you wish to start your own restaurant business and franchise it, then work for a successful franchise restaurant or two, and try to learn everything about the business and why it became successful. If you wish to run a trading company, work for one or, better yet, work for a successful trader. Perhaps you want to open up your own law office. Work for a successful legal firm and emulate the best attorneys. An information technology company? Intern for an up-and-coming information technology firm and learn all you can. The list is unlimited. There is always a place where you can learn in preparation for your future business destiny.

If Jesus did not send out His disciples without training them first, why would you want to start your dream business without proper training? Be patient. The apprenticeship period of your life can take years. Don't leave too early and don't become impatient. My apprenticeship lasted ten years; it may be more or less for you. Learning takes time, and we become more mature and prepared through this period.

According to the Bible, after his conversion, the apostle Paul spent fourteen years in the desert and out-of-the-way places preaching the gospel before embarking on his first apostolic journey. King David learned the good and the bad from King Saul, what he should do and not do, to be a good king of Israel. He observed kingship firsthand. If you listen for God's leading, you will know when to conclude your internship period. I did. Remember, God spoke very clearly to me. You will know fully within your heart when the time has come to move on.

A college degree is important. It gives you a head start in certain businesses. I could not do what I have been doing all my adult life without a chemical engineering degree. But, frankly, the degree itself (five years of study) was like paying an entry fee into the professional club "The Catalyst Industry." Once in, years of learning were still ahead.

Use your employment choices well. We do not have time to waste. Let every employment choice you make be a strategic investment, and view it as a business internship. Do not make lateral moves from one company to another just to make a few extra dollars if it will move you away from your learning environment. Sacrifice immediate benefits for long-term growth.

> *Let every employment choice you make be a strategic investment, and view it as a business internship. Do not make lateral moves from one company to another just to make a few extra dollars if it will move you away from your learning environment.*

If you have a heart for commerce but you aren't sure what business to invest your life in, use your employment choices to check out different fields. No matter where you are or what you are doing in the field of commerce, it is always vital to learn and learn well. Just remember, as a young entrepreneur, you need to complete an internship, so choose your place and type of internship well. It can make all the difference.

Understanding Spiritual Cycles

In the business world, the term *cycle* is used in relation to peaks and valleys of sales and revenues, which are often caused by outside forces like recessions or economic booms. Cycles are understood in terms of dollars, revenues, costs, and economic challenges, but, in God's kingdom, spiritual cycles overarch any natural cycles you may experience. Understanding these spiritual cycles is another key to maintaining your focus and determination to succeed, especially when they take you deep into the valley of challenges.

I want you to understand the spiritual cycles you must go through as a Christian in the world of commerce. It has helped me tremendously to recognize their patterns and learn from them. If you have received a godly promise or a direction for your business life, you will go through the cycles, which are God's way of training us to successfully handle our business venture.

Godly promises follow a clear and specific pattern or cycle before becoming a reality, and we can do little to change it. Learning from these cycles can move you ahead in your journey. The three spiritual cycles God uses are (1) the seeding of the dream in your heart; (2) the journey through the valley of trials; and (3) the sudden fulfillment of the promise. I have experienced all three cycles in my journey to success.

Cycle 1: Seeding of the Dream

Early in the life of a believer, God's ultimate promises and visions for that person are revealed. But this early revelation is only a seed. God impregnates us with the very promise of our destiny, and we are called to nurture and protect that seed until the time comes for it to take root. We are to hold on to the promise and feed it the only thing that can sustain it—our faith.

We have a choice to trust in the vision, accept it, and exercise our faith or reject it as impossible and too far-fetched to ever become a reality. If we accept the vision and receive it by faith, we are set up for the second cycle.

Cycle 2: Journey Through the Valley of Trials

During this journey, our faith in the original promise and vision is tested over and over. We will experience unwanted delays, failures, false starts, brokenness, frustration, and doubt. Our life journey through this valley will take us in almost the exact opposite direction than what we would have expected. Every step during this time will appear to pull us farther and farther away from our ultimate goal. But this is completely in line with the purposes of God and His perfect design.

The Bible is full of examples of these spiritual cycles. Joseph received a dream that, one day, his own father and eleven brothers would bow before him, but first he found himself at the bottom of a well, sold into slavery. Then, just about the time you think he has had enough, a welcome mat is laid out for him at a five-star Egyptian prison! Years go by from the initial dream to the fulfillment, and each step of his journey through the valley of trials appears to push Joseph farther away from his destiny.

Furthermore, God chooses David from among his brothers, at a very young age, to become the king of Israel. Soon after, he experiences victory over Goliath, which seals his call to kingship. However, between that victory and his inauguration as king, David spends years running away and hiding from Saul, living like a bandit and a vagabond. Instead of laying his head on a bed fit for a king, David laid down on dirt and rocks in the caves of Adullam. Instead of being surrounded by attendants and men of character and position, he is surrounded by thieves and men of ill repute. Instead of being with his own brothers and countrymen, which God had promised, David made his home among the Philistines, the Israelites' hated enemy.

I can only imagine what David was thinking when he was forced to live among the Philistines and expected to do their bidding against the Jewish people! He could not have been further away from the promise. Instead of getting closer, it appeared he was drifting farther away.

Let's not forget Moses, Israel's promised redeemer, who rose from the bondage of Egypt. He is given a glimpse of what he is called to do, but instead of rising up with power and influence to lead the Hebrews to freedom, he finds himself in the wilderness for forty years, doing absolutely nothing but shepherding. Imagine being called to lead millions of people as their prophet and leader but then being relegated to managing a herd of sheep for forty years. Our God has a unique sense of humor when it comes to developing kings and leaders.

Cycle 3: Sudden Fulfillment of the Promise

Just like these men of God, just about the time that we are about to give up on our own dream, we enter into the next cycle, which I have termed "the sudden fulfillment of the promise." When the time comes for the promise to be fulfilled, God moves quickly. Unlike the season of trials and waiting, this period is characterized by rapid activity, miraculous events, outpouring of favor, and exponential rise in influence and success. When God wants to move, He moves!

> *Just about the time that we are about to give up on our own dream, we enter into the next cycle, which I have termed "the sudden fulfillment of the promise."*

Within days, Joseph was elevated from sitting in a dungeon to becoming second in command of the entire Egyptian nation, second only to Pharaoh. Suddenly, Saul was dead, and David was crowned king of Israel. After forty years in the desert, Moses was led back to Egypt to confront Pharaoh, declaring the ten plagues on Egypt and, a short time later, leading the children of Israel out of bondage to the edge of the Promised Land.

Spiritual Cycles Today

When I look back at my own life, I can clearly see this exact spiritual pattern. The twelve years of waiting and multiple failures I experienced were not easy on me or my family. I know I had many occasions to doubt if I had even heard the promise of success from God. I remember feeling that it must have been wishful thinking to believe in such promises. As I saw others experience success, I doubted I was even qualified or loved enough to succeed. I would be lying if I told you that I never felt abandoned or forgotten by God. But when I finally experienced success, it came quickly, with my entire financial situation and business success turning around in two swift months.

I can say with great confidence that when we enter the fulfillment phase of promise, the pain of the years when we had to wait and suffer tends to melt away so quickly. Success has a unique way of healing wounds caused by failure. Perseverance, patience, and dogged persistence in pursuit of the promise, and dogged faith in God the Promise-Giver, are the keys to success in the early stages of destiny.

Perseverance, patience, and dogged persistence in pursuit of the promise, and dogged faith in God the Promise-Giver, are the keys to success in the early stages of destiny.

Whether the promise takes one to two or ten to twenty years to be fulfilled, I promise you it will be worth every tear and every failure you experience to reach your destiny. As long as you don't surrender and stop, you will succeed. As long as you make it through the wilderness of trials, you will experience success.

Has God given you a promise to succeed and change your life and even the world? Then hold on to it. Protect it from doubt, unbelief, and the constant attack of those who cannot see how God can use you in great measure. Shield your eyes from what you see currently, and focus on what can and will be. Close your ears to every voice that reminds you of failure and open them to the promise of the Word of God. That is the meaning of faith!

Pray without ceasing! Fight to hang on! Get up and dust yourself off when you fail. Remain resolute in the pursuit of your destiny!

11

TIMING, RISK, AND FAILURE

Timing, risk, failure—three more key principles we must learn on the journey to success. I have seen these principles work in my own journey and the journey of others who have successfully reached their destiny. For the man or woman who is called to the world of commerce, these business keys are critical to success.

You may have heard the phrase "timing is everything." Well, it's true. In business, timing is extremely critical to success or failure. Timing is often associated with pioneering a new concept or business idea, which, to some extent, is true. To be the first company out the door with a product generally means that you will end up capturing most of the market share, and your chance for quick and exceptionally fast growth is much higher.

Timing affects not only new ideas but every aspect of business life. With UNICAT, timing was all about market conditions and the state of the competition. As I mentioned earlier, two years prior to the launch of UNICAT, two low-cost drivers in the catalyst market were bought out by larger competitors, leaving the market underserved, overpriced, and void of real competition. In fact, some oil companies complained of potential behind-the-scenes collusion among the remaining vendors. The market was also void of any new ideas or innovative technology. During this unique window of time, the catalyst industry was ripe for a fresh face with novel ideas and a low-cost economic model. Guess who fit that bill?

Entering the catalyst market four years prior may not have been successful. The low-cost drivers would have still been in the market, and their clients, who ended up becoming our clients, probably wouldn't have switched companies. In addition, the bigger players had not consolidated the market and substantially increased prices. Later, both these steps created the perfect environment for a fresh, new company to enter the competition—UNICAT.

The critical timing for launching our company went beyond those market needs to include the remarkable story of our Chinese suppliers. The companies in China that could supply and support us were available. It was a new market for them, and none of them were aligned with any of our European or US competitors. We had the incredible opportunity to pick the best of more than a dozen potential manufacturing plants.

We partnered with the best Chinese manufacturers, which allowed us to manufacture the highest quality products from the very beginning. In fact, as soon as our competitors figured out our business model, they immediately entered the Chinese market and sought out similar alliances. Many of the remaining plants were bought out by them. But the fact remained that UNICAT was already partnering with "the best of the best" Chinese manufacturers, and timing could not have been more critical.

Whose Sense of Timing Is Perfect?

Considering the perfect timeliness of founding our business, I cannot overemphasize the importance of one fact: God has the perfect sense of time. He applies it to golden opportunities. There was absolutely no way for me to know beforehand the perfect timing for establishing a new catalyst company. Much of this I recognize in hindsight. God knew about every detail of the industry, and He encouraged me to take the plunge at the perfect time.

As God's chosen ones, we need to pray for sensitivity to the Holy Spirit, to His leadings and direction on when move in our lives. Too often, God tells His people to act on a concept or new idea, but fear stops them from moving. How many times have I heard people say that they'd had some idea but somebody else brought it to market? Or they had a chance to buy a piece of land or business a few years earlier, but they got scared, and now it would be worth twice as much?

As God's chosen ones, we need to pray for sensitivity to the Holy Spirit, to His leadings and direction on when move in our lives. Too often, God tells His people to act on a concept or new idea, but fear stops them from moving.

Have you had your own share of missed opportunities? I believe that God constantly drops hints and markers along the way, letting us know when a great opportunity is available and the perfect time to act. We need to listen, and we need to be sensitive, even willing and bold to do so. I wish I could claim that I was always bold and courageous, that I immediately moved on the ideas God gave me, but you already know it didn't happen that way!

I struggled to find the courage to move for almost eighteen months. Finally, God's direct intervention got me to act; otherwise, my opportunity window would have closed. Fortunately, by the grace of God, I moved and obeyed.

Are you going to do the same? Are you going to move out of your comfort zone? Has God been telling you about an idea or opportunity for a while now? What have you been doing about it? Are you sitting and waiting for the right time? Are you preparing and readying yourself? Are you listening carefully for His guidance?

In Scripture, the sons of Issachar were unique because they understood the seasons and times of God: "[They] *knew what Israel should do*" (1 Chronicles 12:32). Understanding the times and seasons of your life is a supernatural gift from God. Pray to the Lord for the spiritual gift of being able to hear what you should do in the pursuit of your destiny.

Yes, there is a time to rest and a time to work, a time to sow and a time to reap, a time to stay still and a time to move. (See Ecclesiastes 3:1–8.) But be ready—keep your eyes, ears, and mind open. God gives out witty and creative ideas to His people all the time. Then, at the proper time, He will call you to act on them. You may not think you are ready, but if He says you are ready, you are ready.

Move, do it in His perfect time, and trust Him, knowing that the One who created time and can see through time will leave nothing to chance!

Rescued from the Edge of Disaster

At UNICAT, we still have occasions when God puts us in the right place at the perfect time to solve a problem, avoid a disaster, or complete an order.

One of these events occurred in the fall of 2013. I rarely go to our main office since I generally work from my ministry offices. When I say rarely, I mean only ten to fifteen times a year. All the preparing of our products to ship them around the world usually happens in our main warehouse in Alvin, Texas.

One day, I decided to go to the main office. I don't even remember why. I just felt an impression to go. As I pulled up to the office, I noticed some of our guys repacking some catalyst into a different container, a common work order for UNICAT. From my car, I thought I saw a puff of dust blow out of the drum that was being repacked, which is not entirely uncommon, but it just didn't seem right.

I walked up to the workers and asked them to repack another drum. As they unloaded it, there, right in the middle, was a massive mound of dust and broken material! I had not seen anything like it in all my years of working with catalyst.

Quickly, the guys grabbed four more drums to repack, and found the same type of debris in all of them. We had over 70 drums lined up to be repacked, and the order was scheduled to be shipped that afternoon to a very important first-time customer. I had all the drums inspected, and more than half contained debris.

I can only imagine what would have happened if that material had been sent to the customer in that condition! The product would have failed quickly if loaded into the unit like that, and it would have been an operational and financial nightmare for everyone involved. I immediately stopped the repacking, changed the lot to an identical one in storage, and made sure the product to be sent out that afternoon was in perfect shape.

As I sat in my office later that day, I realized what a close call the company had just had. Why had I felt the urge to go to the office that morning? Was it a coincidence the drums were being repacked the exact moment I pulled up? Any earlier or later, I would have never seen the dust. And why were they repacking the cartons outside the warehouse that morning when they usually complete repacking assignments inside?

Once more, God's hand of protection was at work. The timing was perfect, and everything was in the right place at the right time for us to avoid an incredible black eye and financial loss. The love and mercy of God for me and this business bring me to tears of gratitude when I think of it. All I can do is thank the Holy Spirit and acknowledge that He was the one who protected the company and me that day. It was a divine act of protection, God's perfect timing, and a two hundred-thousand-dollar miracle! It reminded me that UNICAT belongs to Him.

Understanding Risk

The people of God should not be seen as conservative in nature. Now, I am not talking about anything political. Neither am I talking about being arrogant or proud. However, when it comes to living life, the word conservative is a misrepresentation of a kingly Christian. How so?

Christians should be true risk-takers in society and life. We ought to be the first ones to do things others have not done before, willing to risk failure for the greater glory of the Father, which is exactly what Jesus did when He decided to take on human form and come down to earth to save humanity.

Christians should be true risk-takers in society and life. We ought to be the first ones to do things others have not done before, willing to risk failure for the greater glory of the Father, which is exactly what Jesus did when He decided to take on human form and come down to earth to save humanity. This was a grand risk. If Jesus had failed to fulfill the law and live in perfect obedience, there would have been cataclysmic consequences for all creation. On the other hand, His success meant the restoration of all creation back to Him. That is why Satan took such pains to tempt Jesus forty days in the wilderness, enticing Him to fail. Fortunately, Jesus did not fail, and all authority in heaven and on earth has been laid at His feet. (See Matthew 28:28.)

Too often, Christians are a scared people. Too many live with constant fear of failure and judgment hovering over them. Christians are afraid to speak up against sin because they don't want to sound judgmental. We are fearful of sharing the gospel because we are afraid of rejection. We are so horrified at the idea of being rejected by God that we never seem to rest in our righteousness and the promise of salvation Christ has given us.

In the world of commerce, I see the same thing: Christians who are hesitant to take a bold step for God out of fear of failure. I am convinced we have been designed that way. The Spirit of God that resides in us is one of boldness and courage. The Spirit of the Lion of Judah lives in our hearts.

> *You are from God...and have overcome them; because greater is He who is in you than he who is in the world.* (1 John 4:4 NASB)

This fear rises up in church assemblies as well. Ministers preach in fear of losing their flock, so they water down the Word to soften the blow, but the result is raising timid and weak believers. As ministers, we must be bold with the Word of God, proclaiming it with the intent to create a radical reaction of faith and purpose in believers' heart, even if the Word bruises and cuts the flesh in the process. The bleeding that follows such supernatural wounds leads to life, not death.

Believers who give in to fear never take a bold step of faith to start a business or ministry. They live a life of minimal accomplishment, ceding their purpose and destiny to the enemy of our faith. Young people give in to their emotions and lusts out of fear that they will never have another opportunity to experience what they perceive to be love or a moment of pleasure. All this leads to wrong decisions that scar young lives for years. Godly people commit suicide out of fear of rejection and facing an uncertain future, as if God has abandoned them for good.

Our emotions can vacillate from extreme fear to confidence within minutes. We can go from joy to mourning on a two-step beat. We can be depressed one day and happy the next. No one can build a life or destiny on feelings and emotions; it has to be based on truth, the godly truth that has been planted in us, the truth that comes from the Spirit of God and carries us through rough times. It is the anchor that holds us in the right place when the waves of life try to push us off course.

So here is the fight, the real fight that happens in the difficult phase of your life, when things are not going right, and your purpose is not being fulfilled the way you thought it would be, or when it is taking much longer than you had hoped or believed it would. Fight to hang on, and fight against your emotions. Anchor yourself in what you know that you have heard from God, and what you understand to be true. Every risk has the potential of failure, but the only true failure is quitting. So take the risk with God, stand tall in your faith, and do not give in or give up!

Understanding Failure and How to Use It

Failure—a word that scares so many noble and wonderful Christians from ever trying. We often hear that failure is a part of life but should be avoided at all costs because success is the only experience by which we can measure our worth and fulfillment.

I disagree with that definition of success. Failure is not just an unpleasant part of believers' lives that they must bear a few times whether they like it or not. Failure is a key ingredient and a prerequisite to the success of every believer!

> *Without failure, there will be no fulfillment of purpose and destiny. Without failure, there will be no true growth and maturity. Failure is the key ingredient to growth. It is as important as micronutrients and fertilizers are to agriculture and plant growth.*

Without failure, there will be no fulfillment of purpose and destiny. Without failure, there will be no true growth and maturity. Failure is the key ingredient to growth. It is as important as micronutrients and fertilizers are to agriculture and plant growth. In fact, nature is the perfect example, because natural fertilizers are normally sourced from some of the most undesirable parts of life—namely, death. A living thing dies (a perceived failure) and degenerates and disintegrates. As it does, it can emanate the most pungent odors and produce the most undesirable appearance! Yet death itself and the decomposition that follows fertilize the soil and become the very seeds of life in the cycle of nature.

Death is the ultimate failure and the result of man's fall in the garden of Eden. But in Christ, death is the path to life for those who believe. One cannot happen without the other.

> *Very truly I tell you, unless a kernel of wheat falls to the ground and dies, it remains only a single seed. But if it dies, it produces many seeds.* (John 12:24)

Jesus' death—an ugly death as we all know, the worst of its kind—was the very seed of life for hundreds of millions of others. It is the key to the victory we all share in Him as Christians.

So when you are in a wilderness and trials and failures come your way, embrace them and understand them. Don't dwell on why failure has come or why you have experienced loss; instead, accept failure and loss for what they are, the building blocks of your future success and what build your character as a successful man or woman of God. From what appears to be the death of your dreams or efforts, God can bring newness of life.

Embracing failure and understanding it requires true maturity, but I am afraid that our churches and business schools today do not preach or teach on how to effectively deal with failure.

In some segments of the church, we are taught to expect nothing but absolute assurance that everything will always work out perfectly. When we speak the Word, we expect it will accomplish exactly what we say, and everything will turn out just as you expected. But reality is far from that. Many times, things don't turn out exactly as we hope, and no matter how many times we speak the Word, we don't get the results we want.

Business schools are focused on immediate results, and Western society measures success with a yardstick stick of accomplishments. They do not make any room for failure. Yet failure has great value; the greatest measure of success is how we deal with failure. As business people, I believe we are simply ill-equipped to handle failure.

Most, if not all, of what I have learned in my life has come either from experiencing my own failure or observing how others deal with theirs.

I learned true thankfulness and godly patience from observing one of the greatest men of God I have had the pleasure of knowing, Pastor Kevin Kinchen, as he deals with Lou Gehrig's disease, amyotrophic lateral sclerosis or ALS. I have watched him praise and love God over the past six years even though his body has been failing him.

Furthermore, I learned humility through multiple failed attempts to make business or investments work in those early years when I thought I had it all figured out. I learned my true need for God, and I found my Savior through the entire collapse of my life—socially, financially, and emotionally—as a college student.

I am the sum of my failures and the good decisions I made because of them.

To fail as a Christian businessman or businesswoman is to be assured of success. This is the only way God can keep our god-complex and I-syndrome in check and hope to teach us valuable life lessons we need for growing up and moving from glory to glory.

> *But we all, with open face beholding as in a glass the glory of the Lord, are changed into the same image from glory to glory, even as by the Spirit of the Lord.* (2 Corinthians 3:18 KJV)

The Glory Cycle

Let me draw this simple picture for you. Each glory cycle you enter can turn out one of two ways: Either you are given dreams of success, trials of failure and doubt enter in, you embrace them and patiently persevere to overcome them, and you experience success; or you are given dreams of success, trials of failure and doubt enter in, you don't embrace them, you complain about your circumstances, and then you give up. When we choose the latter cycle, we are placed back at the beginning of our journey in the wilderness, having to circle around again until we learn how to embrace the dark days and difficult moments so that we can experience sudden success.

So where are you in the cycle of your destiny? Have you just come up with that great and crazy idea? The God idea? The dream is now lit in your heart. You are at a great and exciting place in your life. But remember, you must take that risk and, with God's encouragement, overcome the fear. Without risk, there is no success.

The dream is now lit in your heart. You are at a great and exciting place in your life. But remember, you must take that risk and, with God's encouragement, overcome the fear. Without risk, there is no success.

Or are you in the wilderness of your trials? Things are just dark and gloomy. You can't see further than your own circumstances. Problems abound and you feel that you have failed the dream. Whatever you do, don't give up! Rejoice that you are exactly where you need to be because you are going through a prerequisite for success. Your character is being built, and you are being molded into the man or woman of God you ought to be. Seek God's face in prayer and hang on to His Word. Remember, when success comes, it usually comes at the darkest time of our lives—and it comes suddenly.

Perhaps you are enjoying the fruits of success, you are expanding your fortune, and things are going from great to awesome. Enjoy it—you deserve it—but also remember to whom you should give credit. More than that, remember that He brought you to success for an ultimate purpose beyond yourself. Don't forget that He has a plan for you to find your God-given assignment and to use a portion of your resources to extend the kingdom of God wherever He leads you. We grow from glory to glory.

12

THE DOMINION MANDATE

One of the most common statements I have heard from believers in my twenty-four years in ministry is "I don't know what God wants me to do. I want to serve Him, but I have no idea what I am supposed to do for Him. How can I discover what He wants?"

Well, many well-intentioned ministers would simply answer, "Let's pray together for God to reveal this to you" or "The Great Commission is a call on every Christian's life." But for people oriented toward business success, accomplishing goals, and influencing society as a whole, this answer does not cut it.

God has been very clear on what He wants humanity to do. In fact, He spoke it to the great grandfather of us all, Adam, long before a single religious organization was formed.

> *Then God blessed them, and God said to them, "Be fruitful and multiply; fill the earth and subdue it; have dominion over the fish of the sea, over the birds of the air, and over every living thing that moves on the earth."* (Genesis 1:28 NKJV)

These words apply to people of all faiths, beliefs, races, nationalities, and cultures. It speaks of what it means to be a part of the human race and live a meaningful life. It tells us what we need to do to succeed: Be fruitful, multiply, fill the earth, and subdue it.

Once I saw that God spoke these words to the progenitor of the entire human race, I realized a greater depth of meaning and revelation than initially meets the eye. I believe that what we are required to do is explained in the first chapter of Genesis. The message has universal application but especially applies to Christians. We are to be fruitful and multiply.

Producing Good Fruit After Its Own Kind

Everything produces after its own kind. Apple trees produce apples, pear trees produce pears, deer reproduce fawns, elephants reproduce elephants, and humans reproduce humans. This is not brain surgery, but even in its simplicity carries tremendous truth.

Anything that is alive produces, and it will produce its own kind. After all, fruit is the natural reproduction of a tree's DNA and biological makeup. But what does this have to do with a key to your success? *Everything!*

In our businesses, we will reproduce what is in our hearts and minds. The atmosphere that rules our business, the culture that rules the office, the effect we have on our customers, how we produce our products and manage our services—all are fruits we produce every day. What is in our hearts, what occupies our thoughts, and what sits on the throne of our hearts will be reproduced in our endeavors.

One of the most negative fruits produced in abundance in the world of commerce is greed and, unfortunately, it rears its ugly head more often than any other fruit. Greed taking root in your heart is like a nail in the coffin of God-inspired, heavenly designed business ventures. If unchecked, greed will destroy trust between owners and employees, abuse customers, lower the quality of products and services, open us up to reproach and possible litigation, and lead to a loss of customers and departure of high-quality employees.

> *For the love of money is a root of all kinds of evil, for which some have strayed from the faith in their greediness, and pierced themselves through with many sorrows.* (1Timothy 6:10 NKJV)

I think this verse says it best: When we give into greed, we end up piercing ourselves with many sorrows. Greed is a negative fruit of our souls and spirits; in contrast, the fruits of generosity and benevolence build and edify our companies and lives.

> *One person gives freely, yet gains even more; another withholds unduly, but comes to poverty. A generous person will prosper; whoever refreshes others will be refreshed.* (Proverbs 11:24–25)

Fruit Comes From Your Heart

Generosity leads to a flourishing business. It builds unity, trust, and faithfulness within an organization and its employees. It builds trust with customers and brings them back again for additional business. It improves product quality and makes up for failed profit margins with business expansion and additional repeat customers. In the end, it taps into the universal law of all things producing after their own kind. In a company, generosity reaps generous rewards from employees and customers alike.

Many other fruits of behavior can positively affect your company. Patience and grace toward those who make mistakes develop a close-knit workforce that feels like part of a family rather than a group of workers punching a time clock. Truthfulness and honesty in sales produce trust and an incredible feeling of comfort in customers who know that their well-being is your primary concern. They will return again and again.

> *Generosity leads to a flourishing business. It builds unity, trust, and faithfulness within an organization and its employees. It builds trust with customers and brings them back again for additional business.*

Hope and positive faith in the future allow organizations to press through difficult days and cycles and strengthen all who are involved. Sowing profits into good works, and providing assistance to the less fortunate bring purpose and destiny to employees, making them feel part of a greater work than the mere day-to-day affairs of a company. They go from working for an organization to serving an organization. Dealing with customers in humility opens doors for future opportunities. And the fruits go on and on.

You can choose what fruit you produce, but whatever it is, it comes from your heart and mind. True success is measured in more than just dollars and profits. Success is based on the overall health of a work environment, the satisfaction of your customers and employees, the quality of your products and services, your positive effect on society, and the fulfillment and peace you receive from your work.

All of this is the direct fruit of a good and well-intentioned heart. A vital key to success is starting your business venture with the right heart and godly intentions. A good heart check is the best way to know if you are bearing positive fruit and heading in the right direction. When Jim and I founded UNICAT, we prayed that our hearts would be right from the beginning. We desired to serve our families, our customers, and, more so, the kingdom of God. We prayed together over the positives and negatives of the company affairs. We gave generously, building the kingdom of God, and helping the less fortunate in His name. Our purpose was not to financially benefit ourselves alone. We were not profit-driven for the sake of profit alone. We have been blessed to sow and reap good fruit in the world of commerce.

The Art of Multiplication

After producing good fruit, we are to multiply. Remember, Genesis 1:28 (NKJV) says, *"Be fruitful and multiply."* We always think of this merely as reproducing more children on the earth. I believe that God wants us to multiply in other ways as well, reproducing spiritual children and knowledge. One of the keys to success in life and business is learning the art of multiplication or duplication. I want to put this in the simplest terms possible: If you want your business to grow exponentially, you have to multiply or duplicate yourself. Any concept or idea that is to grow rapidly and exponentially has to be readily duplicable and easily teachable to as many people as possible.

> *In the end, whatever the cause, failure to duplicate oneself stunts the growth of a business.*

In the field of commerce, teaching skills and transferring knowledge are lost arts. Sometimes, entrepreneurs or business leaders simply run out of time with all their responsibilities. They feel they have too little time to train someone to be as efficient or savvy as they are.

Other times, it's simply the fear of losing control or not being able to trust people. Business leaders may fear that if they teach others too much, they may just turn around and do it themselves and compete with their mentors.

There is a myriad of reasons why business people are not good at duplication but excellent at driving themselves to the brink of exhaustion by working eighteen-hour days. Fear, poor time management, distrust, overwhelming work schedules, and poor communication or management skills all play a part. In the end, whatever the cause, failure to duplicate oneself stunts the growth of a business. Network marketing or multilevel marketing taps into this duplication concept, and uses it to aggressively grow small businesses in short periods of time.

Multiplication or duplication is a life principle.

Duplication Brings Growth

Anything that is alive naturally grows. Children grow, vegetation grows, and businesses infused with the love, care, and passion of their owners grow. In God's point of view, this growth is measured by how well we have duplicated ourselves within our organization.

I currently have eight full-time salespeople working at UNICAT. Some of my most effective salespeople are those I have personally trained to think, process new information, and close sales the way I do. They are the direct results of training and proper duplication.

I can recall earlier years when UNICAT sales were around five million dollars a year, and I was the only salesperson in our company. I worked twelve-hour days just to keep up. Now, with over thirty-five million dollars in annual sales, I rarely visit customers or prepare sales proposals. In fact, I spend half my time in ministry, and my business is still well managed and flourishing. Why? I have duplicated myself.

Duplication is an art. If done properly, it will transform your business or ministry. Jesus trained twelve men, and eleven of them duplicated His message and purpose, and turned the world upside down! (See Acts 17:6.) Duplication take time, energy, and an investment of oneself, which are hard to come by in our fast-paced world. However, if the system is laid out in a way that duplication is made easy and is acted upon, rapid growth in your company or ministry is assured.

One of your life goals on the road to success should be to teach your salespeople to excel and be more successful than you are. If you have consultants, transfer the highest level of knowledge to them so that they can guide your customers further along than you would have. If possible, structure your company so that it can be successfully duplicated or modeled by others (franchises are one example of this business structure). Allow others to participate in your success by sharing in your idea and using it to create their own success. If you are in the field of teaching, teach others to teach as well or better than you can; if in sports, train athletes to be more skilled than you have ever been. Don't let fear or ego stop you. Leave the success of your business where it has always belonged, in the hands of the God who loves you!

This concept applies in ministry as well. If you are a pastor, raise disciples who can out-preach and out-teach you and who, if allowed to minister on their own, can grow larger and more successful ministries than yours. I think it is fair to say that great teachers of godly principles are truly successful in God's eyes.

Transfer the DNA of success that enabled you to become who you are. Do it intentionally, not passively. Make it a life mission and put in the time necessary to make it work for others. Don't be afraid of losing your leadership or your edge. The art of duplication brings only success in the long run. Father the next generation in your field of endeavor.

> *Very truly I tell you, whoever believes in me will do the works I have been doing, and they will do even greater things than these, because I am going to the Father.* (John 14:12)

13

THE TRANSFER OF WEALTH

The last part of Genesis 1:28 (NKJV) says, *"Fill the earth and subdue it; have dominion."* We call that a "taking dominion" mandate. Two aspects of this mandate are vital for every Christian to understand. One deals with the grand purpose of our lives and why we are building a business, and the other is how we should run our personal and business affairs.

Business is not all about dominating your competition, but it sure is a lot of fun when you do. For a salesman like me, nothing is more rewarding than landing a new account over all your competitors! Competition and the ability to win sales are very natural parts of business. It is healthy and allows us to grow, stretch our resources, and extend beyond our comfort zone.

It is human nature and, frankly, God's nature, to rule. When you start a venture or step into a business, you will eventually rule something. You might be thinking of ruling your market share of an industry or your business may be just a vehicle to support another important project. Either way, you will probably end up ruling that business. Perhaps your highest goal is to accomplish something for the kingdom of God. Even so, you will still need to take dominion over or rule in that specific area.

Let me give you an example: Recently, I met a successful couple who operate a large eldercare company in Australia. The company is thriving, but their true passion is the work they do in Cambodia, rescuing thousands of impoverished children by providing resources and educating them. The business is a vehicle of provision, and the dominion or rule is being established by bringing the kingdom of God to thousands of Cambodian children who have been forgotten in this world. Dominion rule is being established in the streets and cities of Cambodia, where, with God's love, these changed lives are gradually changing society.

As you already know, my businesses became a vehicle to share the kingdom of God with tens of thousands of Muslims, especially Iranians, through ministries we established or fund. Early on, I understood that my mandate was to change a nation and point Muslim societies to Christ.

Let's say God gives you a media-based company and a desire to create a kingdom-based television, Internet, or movie venture. Then you are called to take dominion over the airwaves or whatever portion of media you are called to use. Ultimately, your rule or dominion will take that portion of the media out of the hands of Satan and into the hands of our Father. This is the key—reclaiming fields in Satan's control for the kingdom of God. This should be happening in every

Christian venture or field of commerce. There is no shortage of fields of endeavor that can be affected by kingdom people.

I am convinced that Christians are not called to take possession of wealth or success for its own sake. That is not our ultimate purpose. Making money without a defined target or mission of dominion is not part of God's plan for His people. He has a specific purpose for transferring wealth from one hand to another.

The longer I work as a Christian businessman, the more I recognize the importance of God's mandate for dominion as it relates to the transfer of wealth. Proverbs 13:22 (NASB) says, *"The wealth of the sinner is stored up for the righteous."* This does not mean that we should be out to get other people's money whenever or however we can.

In what ways does this verse find fulfillment in our current world? I believe it is done best through the transfer of wealth using the vehicle of commerce. Commerce is the best way God can transfer wealth from a wicked world to His own kingdom so that the gospel message can be spread throughout the nations. The wealth of the world cannot exchange hands within the church walls alone. We don't want wealth predominately exchanged within the church, from one believer to another.

Commerce is the best way God can transfer wealth from a wicked world to His own kingdom so that the gospel message can be spread throughout the nations. The wealth of the world cannot exchange hands within the church walls alone.

The true transfer of wealth happens in the marketplace, where Christian businesses exchange products and services with those outside of the church, thus bringing the wealth of the world into the kingdom of God. My story is an excellent example of this principle. UNICAT and IRA Consulting are nothing more than a pipeline of wealth transfers from the petrochemical and refining industry into the work of the ministry and world evangelism.

Transfer of wealth occurs when a Christian takes dominion over an area of commerce and accumulates wealth that was once in the hands of Satan and used for worldly purposes. This is exactly what happened when UNICAT finally started making a profit. As we won over new contracts, there was a transfer of wealth from secular companies to Jim McKimmy and me. Through this transfer of wealth, hundreds of thousands of dollars have been invested in the kingdom of God. (I will share more about God's outreach to the nations later.)

By God's grace, we have not only spread the gospel message to tens of thousands of people around the world, but have fed hungry refugees in the Middle East, and supplied water wells to needy communities in Africa. It has been a blessing beyond words to be used to minister God's love to so many people.

This is the purpose of the transfer of wealth. We receive and use money from megacorporations to fund labors of love in the name of Jesus Christ. We pray each day that the Lord will continue to use us in this legal transfer of money from the secular world to God's kingdom.

If you have been called to the field of commerce, you are called to participate in this transfer of wealth. It is a part of your dominion mandate. You are called to take dominion in your niche of the business world, not for yourself alone, but for God's kingdom. The transfer of wealth is ultimately a form of taking dominion if the transfer is intended for a specific purpose that builds and edifies the kingdom of God.

God has shown me that in the very pursuit of our destiny, we end up establishing a micro-kingdom of sorts, which, if properly structured, becomes part of the greater macro-kingdom of God. We stretch His kingdom boundaries by adding our micro-kingdom to His. Most earthly kingdoms in the old days grew by conquest and annexing kingdoms and their territories. But in this case, you are voluntarily and gladly joining your territory to our Father's. We must never forget that we are called to fight and take territory from the world by spiritual force. It is our mandate to be kings and queens, and it is our calling to take as much of the enemy's territory as possible.

> *You are called to take dominion in your niche of the business world, not for yourself alone, but for God's kingdom. The transfer of wealth is ultimately a form of taking dominion if the transfer is intended for a specific purpose that builds and edifies the kingdom of God.*

Taking Dominion in Daily Life

What does it mean to take dominion in our daily lives? Personal dominion begins with ruling our thoughts and emotions. Earlier, I wrote about the importance of not allowing your negative emotions to rule the decisions of your life. A clear mind with a defined purpose is a must for success. Focusing on your goals and purpose is not optional.

Next, personal dominion extends beyond our thought life and actions to our family and business environments. A healthy family with strong relationships will strengthen and provide incredible support for each other in tough times or when we are required to sacrifice time and resources for the business. If you do not have a strong family unit, if your purpose and destiny are not shared, your ventures are on shaky ground. Business vision and purpose must be shared and communicated clearly and lovingly with your spouse and your children. A house divided will not stand in times of trouble. (See Matthew 12:25.)

Next, dominion needs to extend to the environment or corporate culture of your business. A healthy workplace can make a huge difference in the quality of your work and the product and services you offer. Manage and solve intercompany conflicts swiftly and provide resolutions to personnel problems. Nip it in the bud before it grows within the organization. We have had our share of office and personnel issues, and when they remain unresolved, they can make life miserable in the office. A sour office environment affects everyone and manifests itself in the quality of work.

At UNICAT a few years ago, we had an unresolved office problem between one of our primary employees and a partner that lasted too long. As a direct result, we experienced one of our greatest failures in the history of UNICAT regarding a sale to an important customer. That failure cost our company millions of dollars in sales and lost market share. It took four years to recover part of the trust we lost, and I am convinced that the very core of the problem was personnel issues and our failure to take dominion over them swiftly.

You should have a conqueror mind-set.
Short-term and long-term visions need to be set.
There is a market, and it belongs to the enemy.
It is your job to grab it away from him.

This is how the concept of dominion can be extended to the marketplace. No matter what the business venture is, you must be fair but aggressive and remain aggressive to bring growth and expansion. You should have a conqueror mind-set. Short-term and long-term visions need to be set. There is a market, and it belongs to the enemy. It is your job to grab it away from him. In the beginning years of the business, I had a ten-phone-calls-a-day strategy. My goal was to make ten sales calls every single day, day after day. I continued that for two years.

Market share is part of the picture, but there's more to it. Customers' perceptions have to be changed; in other words, their hearts have to be won over. Aggressive marketing and strategies that build on success need to be employed. We are in battle, and time is of the essence. Success builds success, and, when we experience failure, we should deal with it quickly.

Take control of your mind, protect and care for your home relationships, and take charge of your business environment. Mount up on your horse, take your tools of the trade, and charge the enemy's front lines with guns ablaze, without fear or hesitation! Take dominion! It's your mandate!

PART 3:
CHOOSE YOUR ECONOMY

14

CHOOSE YOUR ECONOMY WELL

Most people, Christians and non-Christians alike, have no idea two economic systems are at work in the world today. We are most aware of the secular system, which I call Babylon's economy, which involves incremental rewards, less instead of more, and paycheck-to-paycheck living. The system we are far less aware of is heaven's economy, which involves blessings of exponential rewards, pressed down and overflowing, and living in the freedom of your destiny.

Babylon's economy might seem like an unusual name to you, but Babylonian culture has been in existence for thousands of years. I want to paint a clear picture of who created Babylon's economy, for what purpose, and what it looks like in contrast to heaven's economy. By necessity, you will interact with both economic systems, but it is essential you understand them and can differentiate between them. Choose the right one for your life! Your success depends on it.

The first crucial difference we must recognize is how differently we participate in these two economies. All participation in heaven's economy is by faith in the God of all creation. In contrast, participation in the world's economic system, Babylon's economy, means you have to rely solely on human logic and reasoning. Let's take a close look at this Babylonian system and how it differs from God's economic system.

Babylon's Economy Versus God's Economy

Babylon is a very fitting name for an economic system of governance that sets itself up against the sovereign rule of God. The city of Babylon was built thousands of years ago by a man named Nimrod, the grandson of Ham and the great-grandson of Noah. (See Genesis 10.) In the Bible, Ham was cursed by God for disobeying his father, Noah, by uncovering his nakedness when he had been drunk and for disgracing Noah. As a punishment, Ham's descendants would have to serve his brothers' descendants.

When Nimrod was born two generations later, he would have none of that servitude. He rose to power in the Middle Eastern region people refer to as Assyria, or Mesopotamia. He had a heart of wickedness and a great passion to rule above all others as god.

When Nimrod built the city-state of Babylon, he set out to accomplish his passion: to establish the ascendancy of man and his non-dependency on God the Creator. (Doesn't that sound just like our world today?) The city was to be a resounding testament of man's ability to accomplish the impossible through human effort. The Tower of Babel was the city-state's architectural centerpiece.

Nimrod's reasons for building Babylon were undoubtedly the pursuit of absolute power, mixed with a bit of god-complex run amuck, as well as a deep desire to upend God's prophecy that Ham's descendants would serve their brothers'. So this dominant city-state rose from the desert, and a new economic system that would change how the world viewed commerce, power, and governance was born.

To explain Babylon's economy, I would like to share the four concepts that best describe it: confusion, slavery, incremental rewards, and severe toil. The four cities Nimrod built in the valley of Mesopotamia—Babel (or Babylon), Calneh, Erech, and Accad—represent these four concepts of Babylon's economy.

Confusion Is the Name of the Game—Babel

Babylon comes from the word *babel* which means a scene of confusion or confusing talk. The first thing that can be said about the Babylonian economic system is that it is a voice of confusion; it provides absolutely no spiritual clarity for Christians who seek His kingdom purpose for establishing a commercial enterprise. It is business solely for the sake of creating personal financial gain. It is making money for the sake of making money, power, and position, and giving little regard to anyone else or enlarging God's kingdom on the earth.

Frankly, it is a terrible place for Christian businessmen and women. It leads to confusion, greed, and great conflict. Let me put it this way: the Babylonian system intends to keep God's purpose confounded and believers confused about their destiny. It leads to mediocrity through indecisiveness, lack of direction, or the wrongful pursuit of wealth.

After the Lord spoke to me about starting the company, I procrastinated for eighteen months out of fear and mistrust. I was employing human logic to evaluate my calling. This leads only to fear, paralysis, and babel—confusion. Do you notice that when people become confused, they become essentially paralyzed? They can't make decisions; they are frozen in place, not able to move forward.

Greed, human effort, and human logic best describe Babel. It is a painful place for any Christian to be. Babel provides no clarity; it sets man's own sense of pride in his achievement as the standard-bearer. The business becomes a tower of Babel, telling the world, "Look what I have done with my own two hands!" Babel carries the confusion of the world, and there is no peace in it.

> *The Babylonian system intends to keep God's purpose confounded and believers confused about their destiny. It leads to mediocrity through indecisiveness, lack of direction, or the wrongful pursuit of wealth.*

In contrast, heaven's economy gives Christians purpose-filled lives and a reason to produce profit beyond their own personal pleasure. Business is conducted to honor God, and a portion of the resources are invested into His kingdom. It is an economy of generosity, where greed is rejected, and people's lives are changed for eternity.

Babylon's Economy Brings Slavery—Calneh

Calneh, another one of Nimrod's four cities, actually comes from the root words *kele* and *kala,* which mean "imprisoned" and "constrained." It fits perfectly in the Babylonian system of commerce.

Basically, in this system, we work to enrich others, and our labor builds others' dreams, not our own or God's. We are in a form of slavery or imprisonment. I have seen good men work and slave away 20–30 years for companies just to be told that their job is redundant and their services are no longer required. We trade hours for a set amount of dollars, and we are capped or shut out from a greater return. I realize that having a job that pays well can be a blessing, and

I am not against that. However, men and women of God called into the field of kingdom commerce and entrepreneurship are bound up in chains. They are limited in impact and influence.

You have to leave Calneh or slavery to the world's system to experience freedom and achieve greatness. Truthfully, few people ever achieve financial freedom and true success by working for someone else; many know this is true. Calneh isolates and limits men, and transfers the fruit of their effort and sweat equity to another. Just think of it as the Israelites building the pyramids for the Egyptians. They received sustenance (we describe it as living paycheck to paycheck), but that was it.

This is a choice we have to make at some point. Start-up ventures or businesses are always risky, and the landmines are plentiful, but living in Calneh is much worse. Again, nothing is wrong with working an honorable job, but I don't see how kingdom people can take dominion other than breaking out of the pay-for-your-day system.

Just as the Israelites broke out of their enslavement to Pharaoh and headed into the desert in search of a new future as a free people, we are called to break the yoke of the familiar and predictable cycle of jobs, and embrace the unpredictable yet incredibly rewarding future of kingdom commerce.

Babylon's Limit of Incremental Return—Erech

Erech is the third city built by Nimrod. Its name actually means "incremental" or "measured."

Have you ever heard the phrases "This sounds too good to be true" or "There's got to be a catch"? Often, you hear about a great deal or investment with an incredible return, such as 20 or 50 percent, and the first thought that comes to your mind is, *That just can't be true! Where is the fine print or catch in this deal? This has to be a Ponzi or pyramid scheme.* No one can do that in this economy. If you get 4 percent return, great, and if someone offers you 6 percent, even better! But when you talk about a 10 or 12 percent, or even a crazy 20 percent, return on investment, people just won't believe it! Too many thieves are ready to take advantage of sincere people, "and I am not going to be one of them," you might say. Well, I totally agree with that. I have seen plenty of abuse, even by Christians to other Christians. We are living in a time when a man's word or promise means little and greed has infiltrated everything. Sadly, the church has not been immune to it.

The Babylonian system is designed to give only small incremental increases in our finances. Small raises, small percentages, small increases. For most people in Babylon, except the ones on the top, financial gain comes slowly. Have you felt like something is inherently wrong with putting your money in a bank or stock, and seeing it grow just 2 percent, or growing by 20 percent but then crashing by 20 percent the next year?

We've been so programmed by the Babylonian "Erech" system of incremental return that we find it difficult to believe there is anything better. Jobs are all about incremental return. Banks are all about incremental or, let's be honest, zero return. Most advertised investment accounts are all about incremental return over a long period of time with capital safety as the main driver (which we all know in the world's economy is nothing but a false promise).

In heaven's economy, the Word of God never promises a small incremental return!

On the other hand, in heaven's economy, the Word of God never promises a small incremental return! Look at the promises God has given to Christ's followers:

Give, and it will be given to you. A good measure, pressed down, shaken together and running over, will be poured into your lap. For with the measure you use, it will be measured to you.
(Luke 6:38)

Those are the ones on whom seed was sown on the good soil; and they hear the word and accept it and bear fruit, thirty, sixty, and a hundredfold. (Mark 4:20 NASB)

"Bring the whole tithe into the storehouse, that there may be food in my house. Test me in this," says the LORD *Almighty, "and see if I will not throw open the floodgates of heaven and pour out so much blessing that there will not be room enough to store it."*
(Malachi 3:10)

None of these sounds like a 2 percent, 4 percent, or 6 percent rate of return. These promises look a lot more like exponential return, which is exactly what heaven's economy is based on. Exponential return is an increase that comes more and more rapidly. In God's economy, whatever is sown comes back in far greater measure and faster than in the economy of Babylon. Heaven's DNA is life itself. So whatever is made of pure life cannot help but grow and grow quickly.

Thinking that the world's system is the best you can expect for your financial life is what some would call "stinking thinking." It is all about unbelief or lack of faith in God's economy. Yes, risk is inherent in any venture that can result in exponential return. Faith is a risk, but faith in a living God who has proven Himself faithful over and over again is an extremely well-calculated risk.

When God gives you a business concept that requires an investment of time and money, He is not planning to place you in a long-drawn-out ten-year plan in which you may realize a 10 percent rate of return on your initial investment. He is setting you up for an incredible, unbelievable thirty-, sixty-, hundred-, or even a one-thousand-fold return on your investment. That is the kind of return God promised me if I moved in faith and entrusted UNICAT to Him. He knew that I would use a large portion of that return to expand His kingdom for eternity.

> *God is not planning to place you in a long-drawn-out ten-year plan in which you may realize a 10 percent rate of return on your initial investment. He is setting you up for an incredible, unbelievable thirty-, sixty-, hundred-, or even a one-thousand-fold return on your investment.*

I am currently approaching a five-hundred-fold return on the seed money I invested into UNICAT. Not a bad deal in my book! Honestly, no one is greater than God as a retirement investment strategist! He says give and you will receive, pressed down and running over. (See Luke 6:38.) He says accept His Word, sow seed into His kingdom, and you will receive a return. Why? Because He loves you and because you desire to further His kingdom.

So what does it take? Faith, trust, and some wisdom, of course. I don't advocate doing ridiculous things or throwing your hard-earned capital at every crazy idea or promise that comes your way. I made some really crazy investments in the days of my youth, and none of them worked out as I expected. I don't really regret them though, because they offered a tremendous learning experience. But if I had to do it all over again, I might not repeat one or two of them.

However, I was willing to step out there and invest. The story of the three servants who were given talents as their master leaves for a journey should act as a vivid reminder of how God views proper stewardship. (See Matthew 25:14–30.) I did not want to be like the servant with just one talent, who went and buried it in the ground out of fear. The one who buries talents out of a fear of loss loses everything in the end. It is our responsibility to break out of the Babylonian city of Erech and, by faith, embrace heaven's limitless return.

Babylon's Toil Is Hard—Akkad

Adam's curse for disobeying God and eating of the fruit of the tree of Knowledge of Good and Evil was to toil every day of his life by the sweat of his brow. (See Genesis 3:17.) The earth was cursed, and it would now resist Adam's (and all his descendants') efforts to cultivate it. He had to work hard to get anything out of the earth. Well, not much has changed in the world today. Most people work their tails off to get something out of life.

Every day, people go about their daily work. Many labor vigorously, and they don't have very much to show for their hard work. The Babylonian economic system, exemplified by Nimrod's fourth city, Akkad, is all about resistance that leads to hard labor.

The original earth was designed to cooperate with man. It was meant to produce not just enough but exponentially more than enough from man's effort. When God said, "Be fruitful and multiply and fill the earth" (see Genesis 1:28), He was talking about exponential growth!

Today, the fallen world operates the exact opposite way as it produces significantly less than man's efforts merit. The Babylonian system forces people to work much harder to get a reasonable reward. We live in a cursed system of commerce. The world system is broken and not working as God originally designed it. It needs redemption, just like everything and everyone else.

> *Christ has redeemed us from the curse of the law, having become a curse for us (for it is written, "Cursed is everyone who hangs on a tree").* (Galatians 3:13 NKJV)

To live outside the cursed city of Akkad, you have to believe in the power of God to redeem not only man's life but also the fruit of his labor through Christ. You have to believe that, as Christ's followers, we operate in a new economy—that is, the economy of heaven—which is able to touch and redeem the broken system. We have to be redeemed from the toil of the enemy, Akkad. This means that, even though we work diligently in our field of endeavor, we do not toil just to make ends meet.

You have to believe that, as Christ's followers, we operate in a new economy—that is, the economy of heaven—which is able to touch and redeem the broken system.

God told me that if I trusted in Him, I would make hundreds of dollars for minutes versus pennies for hours I was putting in. I remember the year I worked nonstop every day, including weekends, for forty-two weeks, just to make $52,000.00. This was hundreds of hours of work and travel, and it was tough sales work. It was one of the hardest sums of money I ever made. But now, working in heaven's economy, I have made the same amount of money within a day's work.

I am still working at UNICAT, and I work hard, but I have a lot more to show for it. I am operating in a redeemed environment where the earth and its system cooperate with me and give me a proportionately higher return for the labor I put in. This is not my economic plan, it's God's, and it is explained often in His Word.

So much of God's economy relies on faith, prayer, and the declaration that we will diligently follow God's course for our lives. We need to proclaim that we are redeemed from the curse of Adam. We are free from the bondage of hard labor just to secure a meager harvest, and we operate in faith that our labor will produce a greater harvest than we could ever imagine or dream of—in due season.

Choose Your Economy Well

Are you tired of being confused in your purpose, working and toiling very hard for no return, being imprisoned by a dead-end job, and living in an incremental-return economy where everything takes a very long time to come to fruition? Then break out of Babylon, leave it for good, and never return to it again! Pack your bags and come to the New Jerusalem, the city of God, home of His redeemed people. There, you will experience heaven's economy with clarity of purpose, freedom to pursue your dreams, opportunity galore, exponential return, and rapid progress!

15

HOW NOT TO LOSE FOCUS

Along with success come all-too-common pitfalls, such as complacency, selfishness, or, even worse, pride. After years of hard work, overcoming challenge after challenge, and being pushed to your physical and mental limits, it is natural to take your foot off the gas pedal, rest a bit, and enjoy the spoils of victory. It was no different at UNICAT, and my experience was typical of all entrepreneurs who go through cycles of business growth.

In 2005, about five years after starting UNICAT, we reached six million dollars in annual sales. That was the highest pinnacle I ever expected to reach with the company. I remember telling Jim that if we ever reached this high benchmark in sales, we would know it was a miracle from God's hand. Then we did it!

It may not sound like a lot of revenue, but we were a very small firm with only three full-time employees; our revenues per employee put us at the very top of the industry. Most importantly, we were profitable and making serious money for the first time. We had made a huge leap from our first baby steps in 2001!

Now, this is where the danger can lie. Since we had reached every goal I had set at the start, I became ripe pickings for my human nature to take over and distract me from the greater vision.

At about this time, our distributor, Univar, approached us with an offer to buy us out. Univar and UNICAT—they sounded like they belonged together. Jim was intrigued more than I was about the possibility of selling, but I realized it was an excellent exit strategy. Univar was talking about a valuation of about six million dollars, which meant a three-million-dollar payday for me! I was going to be a multimillionaire! Who could have ever envisioned this happening just three years earlier?

As negotiations became more serious, I got caught up in all the excitement. I didn't sit down and consider the reasons we launched the business in the first place. What about God's vision for UNICAT and His plans to promote the gospel in the Middle East through the company? Was I going to invest the proceeds from the sale into the ministry? What would a thirty-nine-year-old man with boundless energy do once the sale was complete? Retire or go into full-time ministry? Wouldn't I need the funds from the sale to retire on?

In the heat of the negotiations, I wanted to cash out and figure the rest out later. It was a selfish decision, with my own needs outweighing the needs of the kingdom of God. I had simply lost my focus. I could not see beyond my original dream to what the Lord had planned for the work. This is a bad place for any businessperson to be, especially for believers in Jesus Christ.

As destiny would have it, Univar's board did not approve the purchase of UNICAT in the final negotiations. What a shock for all of us! Jim and I were so disappointed. Everyone had been 100 percent certain that this deal was locked up. As the smoke cleared, we both had time for some serious reflection.

Had God intervened and prevented the sale from going through? Could that be possible? Of course, in hindsight, I know for certain that God intervened. Today, with over thirty-five-million dollars in annual sales, the company is worth much more than six-million dollars. By God's grace, it has done a lot more for the kingdom than it could have if we had sold it years ago.

Don't Fall Short of the True Goal

Some Christians may bank on the idea that God is working on their behalf just to financially bless them, but this falls far short of His true goal. Yes, of course the Father wishes to bless His children, but there is a much greater purpose for it all. We are called to serve in the same spirit as His Son Jesus Christ, who set the perfect example to all believers by putting the Father's will first before His own. Keeping UNICAT was both for my own good and the betterment of God's kingdom. God intervened because He knew I could not see beyond myself and my little world. I am convinced that we perceive little of God's grand view for our lives.

If left to our own accord, we will accomplish little. We will get off at the first rest stop we find on the road to our kingly calling. Univar's purchase offer was my very first rest stop, and I wanted to get out and stretch my legs. But God had bigger plans for us, and, fortunately, we serve a God who cares for us so much that He will not leave us to our own accord.

I remember Jim and me talking just a few years later when the company's sales had reached ten million. What fools we would have been to sell it to Univar! We were thanking God for His intervention, even though we'd had a nice little pity party when the sale fell through.

My word of caution to anyone who is called into commerce and starting a business is to never take your eyes off the prize. Do not get distracted by your own needs. Start looking at the things you can do with the proceeds of the business. Imagine the good you can do, the lives you can change, and the affect you can have, especially since more influence comes with more success.

Do not get distracted by your own needs. Start looking at the things you can do with the proceeds of the business. Imagine the good you can do, the lives you can change, and the affect you can have, especially since more influence comes with more success.

You would think that I learned my lesson, but no, we are creatures of habit and inherently selfish. As the company grew, so did the temptation to sell it at a higher price. In 2012, a very large catalyst firm approached us and offered $28 million for the company. Not a bad day at all and extremely tempting!

By this time, UNICAT was twelve years old. I was older and had done a fair amount in the ministry with the proceeds from the business. It made perfect sense, the fairy-tale ending, the last chapter to the great miracle called UNICAT. So we tried to sell, and did we try!

For eight months, we negotiated. We did everything the buyers wanted, and had meeting after meeting, but in the end, the sale did not go through. The buyer changed the nature of its offer right at the last minute. In so many ways, this was a crushing blow, especially to Jim, who was ten years older than me and already successful in his own right. Jim helped to found UNICAT to bless me and to obey what the Lord had asked him to do. He felt that he was ready to move on from catalyst work.

I believed I had an unfinished assignment, but Jim felt that he had fulfilled his. In so many ways, it was true. The outreach to Muslims was my calling, not his; it was my assignment for life. Jim had his own dreams and visions. This failure to sell the company was extremely hard on him—more than I realized. Suddenly, it dawned on me that Jim would inevitably retire one day and leave our partnership. I had to face the reality of running the company without my best friend standing next to me. The thought scared me, and I knew it would be inevitable.

By then, I knew that keeping the company was more like bearing a cross for him, and it was turning out to be a burden for me as well. I was tired and felt like I had nothing more to offer to the vision. The company had already reached levels beyond my wildest dreams. We had accomplished so much that I felt like I had nothing more to add. But this is exactly where spiritual maturity comes into play.

An Action at the Crossroads

We had to choose what course of action we were going to take: quit trying to expand, and reduce the size and complexity of the company (it would still be successful as a smaller operation with profitability for years to come) or continue to do what we had always done—grow, succeed, and make the company more profitable.

To me, the decision was inherently a choice between being servant-minded or self-minded. To reduce the size of UNICAT and make the company profitable enough to maintain a reasonable income for all owners made sense to our worn-out bodies and minds. Working seventy to eighty hours a week can wear you out over twelve years, and I was experiencing an acute case of OFS, or Owner Fatigue Syndrome. However, succumbing would have been inherently selfish. We are called to be servants in the image of the greatest of all servants: Jesus Christ.

> *Who, being in very nature God, did not consider equality with God something to be used to his own advantage; rather, he made himself nothing by taking the very nature of a servant, being made in human likeness. And being found in appearance as a man, he humbled himself by becoming obedient to death—even death on a cross!* (Philippians 2:6–8)

Being servant-minded is exactly that—thinking of the needs and wants of others far more than your own. This is not a natural thought process for human beings in general, and it becomes almost antithetical to the psyche of successful businessmen and businesswomen who have paid the price to be prosperous and financially secure, and want to start enjoying the fruits of their labor.

The Strength to Stay the Course

What gives us the strength to stay the course and keep focus? The Spirit of God who dwells in all who believe. The same Spirit who led Jesus to leave the highest position of all creation to come to the lowest position known to man—serving man and washing his feet—dwells within us. As a Christian businessman, I had to figure out who I was serving and for what purpose I was laboring.

A truly successful businessman understands he is a faithful servant to his customers and employees. More than that, he understands that he is ultimately serving the master, Jesus Christ, and His Father, and that their will always supersedes his will.

It was obvious that God had blessed us, and with all my heart, I believe God spoke to me, *This is not the end of the journey for you and UNICAT, Mani. I want your focus to be on serving my kingdom and reaching the lost in the Muslim world.*

Jim and I came to an agreement. We were being called to take a closer look at what a larger, more powerful UNICAT with higher profitability and influence could do in the world for the kingdom of God. It was clearer than ever that UNICAT had never been about

Jim and me; it had always been about God. It may seem like an unusual way of looking at a successful business, but we saw that it was about something greater than us and beyond our own limited vision. We decided not to look for a new buyer. Instead, we chose to carry our crosses by continuing to run the company.

This is not easy when your flesh desires to stop, but the Spirit has much to do and God's kingdom needs as many successful kings as it can get. A servant-minded king is the best of all kings. He not only grows the boundaries of his kingdom by aggressive warfare and conquest, he secures his victories and all he has attained by serving his subjects well and building confidence in them that he has their best wishes in mind.

This is how Jesus operated, and we are to operate in the same manner. We ought to understand that it is our mantle and our calling to enter the world of commerce and, by aggressive effort, build successful enterprises and businesses. Even after we achieve success, we need to understand that we are never far from our servant identity. We should perceive our success as a vehicle to serve God and His people. He comes first and, ultimately, His kingdom, not ours, matters.

We must also come to grips with the fact that the people God entrusts us with matter, both employees and customers. When we take good care of them, we glorify God and secure spoils for His kingdom for years to come. We are bound to serve something far greater than ourselves. It is not about you or me, it is all about Him.

16

KEEP ON DIGGING

By now, it is clear that God has provided countless spiritual lessons in His Word to help His people, Christians like you and me, on their journey to success. There is a fascinating account in the Old Testament that gives us a clear picture of God's success plan for His people. It is the story of Isaac and his journey from the land of the Philistines to Beersheba in Israel. On the surface, it seems to be just another story about a Bible hero, but it is far more than that. It is a step-by-step guide to success for an individual called by God. More importantly, the events in this story mirror the way God leads Christian people in business today. I truly believe Isaac's story teaches us that we can learn the specific path God will take us to fulfill our individual destiny. I can assure you it was the path He led me on through the UNICAT story.

Isaac's story began with a promise. He was facing a severe famine in the land God had promised to him, just as his father Abraham had faced. Isaac was being forced to choose whether to stay in the land that was promised to his father's descendants or to leave. God told Isaac not to leave, and reminded him of the promise He had made to him, his father, and generations to follow.

> *Now there was a famine in the land—besides the previous famine in Abraham's time—and Isaac went to Abimelek king of the Philistines in Gerar. The* Lord *appeared to Isaac and said, "Do not go down to Egypt; live in the land where I tell you to live. Stay in this land for a while, and I will be with you and will bless you. For to you and your descendants I will give all these lands and will confirm the oath I swore to your father Abraham. I will make your descendants as numerous as the stars in the sky and will give them all these lands, and through your offspring all nations on earth will be blessed, because Abraham obeyed me and did everything I required of him, keeping my commands, my decrees and my instructions.* (Genesis 26:1–5)

God gave Isaac a promise. Every journey starts with a promise and a dream. This story is just like our own. We all carry within us dreams for the future that give us hope and comfort, but we also experience seasons of famine. Minimal provision, a myriad of financial struggles, long delays, lack of direction, and really tough circumstances define these seasons of famine.

This is when people often give up and run away to Egypt, which appears to be the easy way out. Now, Isaac was living in Gerar (modern southern Israel), the land promised to his father, but it was under the rule of Abimelek, king of the Philistines. The king was not a friend of Isaac or a believer in the God of Abraham, and he did not recognize that the land was promised to Abraham and his seed. Isaac had a promise, but it was in the hands of his enemy. We often face this situation at the beginning of our journey.

> *God plants us in our destiny early on, long before we ever become prosperous and successful in it.*

God plants us in our destiny early on, long before we ever become prosperous and successful in it. If in business, we are placed within a field of commerce, and we get a sense that, someday, we are going to make it in the very same field of work. Or maybe we are planted in a field of study that we will one day master. Whatever or wherever it may be, we will find ourselves in our destiny but ruled by others. This may mean we have to work for someone else for a while or labor for the unknown for a time. During this season, we experience a long drought of our dreams. But God will remind us of our purpose as often as needed to keep us on course. Our job is to not give up on our dreams and run away to Egypt.

Trust God and stay put! Don't leave the land of promise. God has promised it to us for a reason!

Isaac and Abimelek

> *So Isaac stayed in Gerar. When the men of that place asked him about his wife, he said, "She is my sister," because he was afraid to say, "She is my wife." He thought, "The men of this place might kill me on account of Rebekah, because she is beautiful." When Isaac had been there a long time, Abimelek king of the Philistines looked down from a window and saw Isaac caressing his wife Rebekah. So Abimelek summoned Isaac and said, "She is really your wife! Why did you say, 'She is my sister'?" Isaac answered him, "Because I thought I might lose my life on account of her." Then*

> *Abimelek said, "What is this you have done to us? One of the men might well have slept with your wife, and you would have brought guilt upon us." So Abimelek gave orders to all the people: "Anyone who harms this man or his wife shall surely be put to death."*
>
> (Genesis 26:6–11)

You must be wondering how this Bible account could possibly apply to your life today. Well, there is a lot to be said about Isaac lying to Abimelek. He actually repeated the mistake his father had committed while in Egypt, when he lied about his wife and Isaac's mother, Sarah. We often repeat the mistakes of our parents in our lives. This is a real struggle and a significant challenge for upcoming entrepreneurs and dream-chasers. They have to overcome not only external challenges and pressures but enemy number one, who influences them from within.

The fact is that we are products of our environment and upbringing. If no one else in our family has experienced real success or achieved much, we may have to constantly convince ourselves that we can do what they have not. We must be aware that we are quite capable of sabotaging our future by repeating the same mistakes or following the same patterns of decision-making as those close to us. Often, we must fight negative thinking to overcome deep-seated fears of failure and poor life practices picked up along the way. Ninety percent of the battle to keep from falling into the trap of mediocrity is to recognize our weaknesses so that we can overcome them with the help of the Lord.

But there is good news! Although Isaac committed the same mistake as his father—which could have cost him everything, including his wife—God delivered him by giving him favor with Abimelek. The Lord spares Isaac's life and gives him a second chance to redeem himself and remain in His purpose. We serve a merciful God, a heavenly Father of grace, who will not let us down despite our many errors.

Of course, we have a role to play in this journey. I am not suggesting that we kick back and not work to put our best foot forward for the Lord. We ought to minimize mistakes, correct poor habits, work diligently, and let go of timidity and fear. Above all else, we must keep a humble and gentle heart toward Him. Then we can rest in the truth that God is faithful and merciful, and that He covers our numerous mistakes on the way to success.

I have made and continue to make a fair share of blunders, and I am still amazed at how God covers me with His love and forgiveness, leading me on to greener pastures despite my failures. He is a faithful Father.

> [Be] *confident of this very thing, that He who has begun a good work in you will complete it until the day of Jesus Christ.*
> (Philippians 1:6 NKJV)

Pushed Out of Our Comfort Zone

> *Isaac planted crops in that land and the same year reaped a hundredfold, because the LORD blessed him. The man became rich, and his wealth continued to grow until he became very wealthy. He had so many flocks and herds and servants that the Philistines envied him. So all the wells that his father's servants had dug in the time of his father Abraham, the Philistines stopped up, filling them with earth. Then Abimelek said to Isaac, "Move away from us; you have become too powerful for us."* (Genesis 26:12–16)

Now here this is a very interesting part of the story, which I call being pushed out of your comfort zone. Isaac had to leave Gerar, where he was raising his family and where he had prospered. He had to move away from the Philistine city and travel deeper into the Promised Land. But Isaac didn't like the change, and, generally, neither do we.

Right before our journey is about to begin, we usually have to be nudged or, in my case, seriously pushed out of our comfort zone. It is purely human nature to like comfort; when we find a place of comfort, we want to remain in it indefinitely. Change is never easy, and we typically don't do well with any form of it. Just look at Sunday morning church services—you can pretty much guess where everyone will be sitting at every service. There is just something about a comfort zone that makes us want to cuddle up inside it and not come out.

When I worked for the recycling company, I struggled with the decision to stay or to leave and start UNICAT. It got progressively harder for me every day. When I heard, *Pack up your bags and resign today,* I had no doubt I had heard from God. It was time to leave. I was being pushed out of my comfort zone!

So many difficult things happen in our lives. We may get laid off or lose someone we depend on. Other times, God may push us out into an open field. It is never too late to pursue your destiny, and God is quite patient. When the time comes, if you have not moved yet, He may just slip right behind you, and give you that big push you really need!

It is never too late to pursue your destiny, and God is quite patient. When the time comes, if you have not moved yet, He may just slip right behind you, and give you that big push you really need!

I recently talked to an old friend who had been laid off after working twenty-one years in sales for an environmental mold remediation company. He is a good man of God, with a huge heart, and an exceptionally good salesman. When we spoke, he was really down and depressed. He could not believe that he had been let go after so many years, and he saw no chance of being hired by anyone else at his age.

But I saw an opportunity. He had the contacts, he had the knowledge and the work ethic, and all he needed was a push to start his own business.

"Why aren't you starting your own company?" I asked him.

"That's simple," he answered. "I don't have the financial backing to complete the jobs."

I responded, "All these years, you have made millions of dollars selling for others. Now, it's time you put that knowledge to work for you, and use your new success to bless the kingdom of God! Go start your company, line up the jobs, and I will be your financial backer."

To say he was elated would be an understatement. It suddenly clicked for him that there was hope and a plan in motion. All he had to do was to go with it, and trust that God would make it all work out. I am certain that all the years he had apprenticed for his mold remediation company have made him more than able to build a successful company of his own. All he needed was a push out the door into an open field.

The Lord Will Make Room for You

Isaac left the false comfort of life with the Philistines, and moved his family, cattle, and all his possessions to the land specifically promised to his father.

> *So Isaac moved away from there and encamped in the Valley of Gerar, where he settled. Isaac reopened the wells that had been dug in the time of his father Abraham, which the Philistines had stopped up after Abraham died, and he gave them the same names his father had given them. Isaac's servants dug in the valley and discovered a well of fresh water there. But the herders of Gerar quarreled with those of Isaac and said, "The water is ours!" So he named the well Esek, because they disputed with him.*
>
> (Genesis 26:17–20)

So, just like Isaac, perhaps you step into your journey and think everything is going to go well for you and according to plan. Not! You will face contention and quarrels. There will be resistance from all sides. First, there is the natural resistance and challenges that come with starting any new venture. No one likes to buy from someone they never heard of, and how do you pay bills when you don't have any money coming in? Then you have the added bonus of being a kingdom-based company, so you get the devil's negative attention too. He is not going to like what you are up to. Certainly, your success means that the wealth of the wicked is going to pass to the righteous, and Satan does not want to see that happen.

You will have natural and spiritual resistance. Physical and spiritual warfare broke out all around UNICAT those first two years. Contention and quarrel were the names of the game. Notice that Isaac did not stop digging wells, and I didn't either. When a well is stopped up, go dig another one!

> *Lazy hands make for poverty, but diligent hands bring wealth.*
> (Proverbs 10:4)

> *Then they dug another well, but they quarreled over that one also; so he named it Sitnah. He moved on from there and dug another well, and no one quarreled over it. He named it Rehoboth, saying, "Now the LORD has given us room and we will flourish in the land."* (Genesis 26:21–22)

If you continue to dig wells, and don't give in to your emotions to quit, you will come to an open field, where you can grow, multiply, and prosper without resistance and hindrance. There is a place where every venture moves from concept to reality, from possibility to inevitability, from hardship to fulfillment.

> *From there* [Isaac] *went up to Beersheba. That night the LORD appeared to him and said, "I am the God of your father Abraham. Do not be afraid, for I am with you; I will bless you and will in-*

> *crease the number of your descendants for the sake of my servant Abraham."* (Genesis 26:23–24)

At last, Isaac arrived at his open field, and established himself in the land that had been promised to him. Yet the blessing did not end there; in fact, he had an encounter with God Himself at a place of meeting. The Bible says that Isaac actually dug another well as a sign of worship and thanksgiving.

Know this: If you pursue your godly assignment, trusting in Him when He launches you into your destiny, and remaining diligent through the initial cycles of resistance and contention, you will not only be blessed with success but will have an encounter with God in which He will establish you once and for all in your divine purpose. This will be a seal of affirmation from God Himself that you and your seed will be continually blessed because of your obedience to Him. Our pursuit of a vision and its fulfillment touches not only us but also generations to come. The ultimate purpose of any godly endeavor is to come to a place of meeting where we are planted securely in our purpose and live no more in a place of struggle. Then we can drink out of the well of thanksgiving and plenty in our own promised land. This is the way God intended it to be.

17

STAND STRONG IN BATTLE

In everyday life, we encounter physical and spiritual battles. There will be battles in our workplace, in our marriage, and in our friendships. The battles do not mean defeat by any means. They are meant to make us stronger, and to increase our understanding of God's purposes for us on this earth. Jesus told us clearly, *"In the world you will have tribulation; but be of good cheer, I have overcome the world"* (John 16:33 NKJV). What happens if the battles are really strong? What if, beyond digging wells, we have to fight for every last step of the road on our journey? What if the enemy we are fighting against is the strongest one of all—Satan?

I have found inspiration and guidance from a biblical account in which Israel fights against a strong enemy. It will inspire you to face your battles and win!

> *The Amalekites came and attacked the Israelites at Rephidim.*
> (Exodus 17:8)

Amalekites! These guys show up in Israel's history over and over again, and they're notorious for being the enemies of God's people. They were vicious aggressors and simply just bad news. Their origin dates back to the very first nations after the Flood, so they were an ancient enemy. Shortly after Israel was rescued from the bondage of Egypt, they had to face down the Amalekites, who attacked them in the desert in a place called Rephidim.

I am convinced that right after we make the decision to break away from the bondage of our own Egypt—to break free into our destiny in the Lord—we will engage in a fierce battle with an old enemy. In the field of business, your "Egypt" or bondage might be doubt, fear, hesitation, or the tiresome rut of a dead-end job—anything that keeps you from pursuing the best that God has for you in Jesus Christ.

In this account with the Israelites, the Amalekites are people who have given themselves over to pure evil. I see the Amalekites as representing the city of the world versus the city of God, Israel. In this interpretation, the Amalekites represent the oldest enemy of God's people—Satan.

The location of the battle with the Amalekites is important, too. It is called Rephidim, where the Israelites camped in the wilderness, but no water could be found there, and it led to a quarrel with Moses. (See Exodus 17:1–3.) When the people of Israel complained about the wilderness, Moses asked them, *"Why do you put the LORD to the test?"* (Exodus 17:2).

In every worthy pursuit is a time and a place where no provision can be found. This usually occurs at a time when provision is really needed. In commerce, people usually hit a "Rephidim" during an initial start-up, when resources are scarce, and our internal enemies, fear and doubt, seem overwhelming. We look around, desperately in need of some water (provision), but none is to be found. Our natural tendency is to grumble and complain to God and those around us.

In every worthy pursuit is a time and a place where no provision can be found. This usually occurs at a time when provision is really needed.

Right about this time, when fatigue and weakness have set in, we become prime targets for Satan to attack. Our ancient enemy is very good at stealing and destroying God's people and their dreams through doubt and unbelief. (See John 10:10.) We get tired of fighting for survival, barely keeping our heads above water. If we give in to the temptation to grumble and complain, we leave the door wide open for the enemy to come and make a frontal assault on our plans.

In Rephidim, in response to Moses' prayers, God provided the miracle of water rushing out of a rock, meeting the desperate needs of the Hebrew people. In almost all circumstances, when you are walking in your destiny and doing what you are called to do, and you step into your desert in faith, God will supernaturally meet your needs, especially when you hit your dead-end Rephidim spots along the way.

Our Weapons for Victory

Remember that there are multiple Rephidims or dry spots in our initial journey to success. We need to recognize them for what they are—critical moments when the life and death of our business hang in the balance. The Lord has provided supernatural weapons to use against our enemy so that we can be victorious overcomers.

The first key to overcoming is to stay focused in what you are doing and where you are heading (keep the goals and purposes in front of you at all times). The second key is to fight the temptation to give up with every bit of faith you have in God and His Word. You can call on His assistance to strengthen your faith like the little boy in the gospel of Mark: *"Lord, I believe; help my unbelief!"* (Mark 9:24 NKJV).

As business people who trust and believe in God, we have a unique ally on our side who exists completely outside of our own intellect and resources. We can bring the Spirit of God to bear. Additional weapons for the battle include taking counsel from His wisdom, seeking His face, searching His Word, and praying often. Remember, *"the weapons of our warfare are not carnal but mighty in God for pulling down strongholds"* (2 Corinthians 10:4 NKJV).

While Israel battled with swords and spears, we fight a spiritual war with prayer, praise, and the declaration of God's Word over our minds and lives. We are fully equipped with all the spiritual resources we need to win this vital battle for our mind and emotions. Giving up is a decision. Under severe external pressure and stress, giving up is the easiest thing to do, waving the white flag of surrender. I know this all too well. I almost quit UNICAT multiple times during the first two years. I had moments when I felt I had given it my all, I had tried to the best of my ability, and it was just not working. By God's strength, I endured the battle and didn't give up.

Find Others to Stand by You

The dry seasons are just that—dry. There is no money and no success, and God seems absent. In my dry season, Satan was never too far away. Right there, whispering in my ear, he'd tell me, "You did your best. You gave it your best shot. It just didn't work out!" He would mock, "Quit and go back to work for someone else so you can at least pay your bills. What are you doing here in this desert?"

What held me together was my faith, God's Holy Spirit, and a "Joshua" who held my hands up until I made it through to victory. My Joshua, who gave me unmitigated support, was my partner, Jim McKimmy.

> *It is very important to have a good support structure around you. You need successful men and women who love God, who understand business and its nuances, and who are godly, principled people who have your best interests at heart. They will stand by your side when things are not going well and will do what is necessary to help you succeed.*

It is very important to have a good support structure around you. You need successful men and women who love God, who understand business and its nuances, and who are godly, principled people who have your best interests at heart. They will stand by your side when things are not going well and will do what is necessary to help you succeed. I can say without any doubt that I would not be here if it wasn't for Jim. He pushed me through those difficult first years and provided vital encouragement when success was in short supply, and there were ample sand dunes in the desert of failure all around me.

Satan will never cease trying to abort a godly destiny. He will attack you at your weakest point, and will continue to do so at every turn and opportunity that presents itself. But we can stand on the Bible's declaration *"greater is He who is in you than he who is in the world"* (1 John 4:4 NASB). This promise of God will take us through the driest times in our journey through His kingdom.

18

WHAT IS YOUR ASSIGNMENT?

What if you still aren't sure what your assignment is from the Lord? How will you find it? I believe that God will use the everyday circumstances of your life and your employment to speak to your heart. He will woo you or nudge you in the direction you can serve Him best. He will let you know what area of commerce you are called to and, beyond that, what ministry in which you will effect the greatest change in the world for the kingdom of God.

I'm grateful that the Lord gives us examples from His Word on how to live our lives, examples of people who have successfully walked paths very similar to what we walk today, even though they are from many centuries ago. Most Christians are very familiar with the Old Testament account of David as king of Israel, how God chose him to be king and had the prophet Samuel anoint him for the throne years before his kingship. You may have heard countless teachings about David, and the lessons we can learn from his journey through life.

However, not many have heard success stories about the king who reigned before David—Saul. You might be surprised to learn that God has given us a very interesting account of how He led Saul to his kingdom assignment. It provides a good lesson in how God can lead us as well. The lesson is based on the early account of Saul and his rise from an average citizen to the king of Israel. It is clear how God calls us and then dispatches us to discover our ultimate destiny. We all know that, in the end, Saul did not fulfill the destiny God had in mind for him, but the Lord still called him in the beginning. I believe we can all learn about being called by God from this example.

> *God prepares and even reveals our purpose to us before we reach any level of success. All these God-led steps of our journey—being called, being set aside, being anointed, being sent out—happen before we even realize the specifics of our calling.*

God prepares and even reveals our purpose to us before we reach any level of success. All these God-led steps of our journey—being called, being set aside, being anointed, being sent out—happen before we even realize the specifics of our calling. Still, very early in our journey, God reveals our destiny and purpose, and then launches us to conquer the land of our heavenly promise.

Although King Saul has always been a footnote in the life of David, one of the greatest figures in the Old Testament, his rise to the throne of Israel is full of kingship identity truths that apply to our own lives. Saul's election and rise to kingship could not have been more inconspicuous and peculiar.

> *Now the donkeys belonging to Saul's father Kish were lost, and Kish said to his son Saul, "Take one of the servants with you and go and look for the donkeys."* (1 Samuel 9:3)

Yep, the prelude to Saul's meteoric rise to power and kingship authority was the glorious task of searching for a bunch of lost donkeys. The man set out on a mundane task to fix a family financial problem, and ended up being anointed the king of all Israel. How is that possible? Well, in God's universe, rising from obscurity to fame is one obvious way to get elected to higher office.

> So [Saul] *passed through the hill country of Ephraim and through the area around Shalisha, but they did not find [the donkeys]. They went on into the district of Shaalim, but the donkeys were not there. Then he passed through the territory of Benjamin, but they did not find them.* (1 Samuel 9:4)

How Lost Donkeys Work Their Magic

Have you ever looked back at your life before meeting Christ? Have you considered how you got yourself into the mess you were in? Problems all around you, no solutions in sight—no matter where you went or what you did, you couldn't find a way out. I have coined a name for all the problems we face that lead us to the cross: lost donkeys. Some have one, and some, like Saul, have a bunch of lost donkeys trotting around. But in the end, they lead us to the only person who can truly help us—Jesus Christ.

Saul decided that he'd had enough of chasing donkeys and was ready to return to his father's house. In this story, Samuel the prophet points Saul to Jesus. Let's continue to read:

> *But the servant replied, "Look, in this town there is a man of God; he is highly respected, and everything he says comes true. Let's go there now. Perhaps he will tell us what way to take."*
>
> (1 Samuel 9:6)

Well, that pretty much sums it up. Somehow, somewhere, there is a solution to every problem, and that solution leads humanity back to God. The lost donkeys of our lives are doing their job—running away, hiding, and making sure we don't find them on our own. We are forced to give up or seek a man of God. Well, who better to seek than Jesus Himself?

> *As they were going up the hill to the town, they met some young women coming out to draw water, and they asked them, "Is the prophet here?" "He is," they answered. "He's ahead of you. Hurry now; he has just come to our town today, for the people have a sacrifice at the high place."* (1 Samuel 9:11–12)

What we don't realize is that God is using our lost donkeys for a greater purpose than we could ever imagine. He is using them as a divine setup to get us to come to Him. In fact, He sets Himself up to be exactly where we search for our answers. He actually arrives there ahead of us. It should not surprise anyone who has placed their faith and trust in Jesus that everything that occurs before that providential moment is part of a series of events—like links in a chain—that ultimately lead us to Him and to our calling.

> *They went up to the town, and as they were entering it, there was Samuel, coming toward them on his way up to the high place. Now the day before Saul came, the Lord had revealed this to Samuel: "About this time tomorrow I will send you a man from the land of Benjamin. Anoint him ruler over my people Israel; he will deliver*

> *them from the hand of the Philistines. I have looked on my people, for their cry has reached me." When Samuel caught sight of Saul, the* Lord *said to him, 'This is the man I spoke to you about; he will govern my people.* (1 Samuel 9:14–17)

Now, ask yourself one question: What did Saul ever do to be qualified as God's answer to the cries of His people? What war did he wage or what battle did he win? What enemies of Israel did he defeat to be elected the ruler of Israel? What did he accomplish? Absolutely nothing!

There are no records of any previous exploits of Saul in the Bible. We find him mentioned for the first time in this chapter, and his story begins as a young man simply looking for a herd of lost donkeys. So what qualified him to be a king? Saul was elected and qualified by God to be the next ruler. The One who elects and promotes is the One who matters. His choice is final; it's the only one that counts.

> *We are given a calling far greater and higher than our most elaborate imaginations, far above and beyond where our dreams can ever take us.*
> *Our perception of ourselves can't possibly reach as far and as high as God's view of us, and how great He believes we can become.*

The beautiful picture we see here is that we are no different from Saul. We all are running around looking for our own lost donkeys, and out of nowhere, we meet Jesus who, unbeknown to us, has chosen us to be kings and rulers in this world. He sees in us what we don't see in ourselves, and He knows us in ways we can't imagine. We are given a calling far greater and higher than our most elaborate imaginations, far above and beyond where our dreams can ever take us. Our perception of ourselves can't possibly reach as far and as high as God's view of us, and how great He believes we can become.

Interestingly, when Samuel and Saul first met, the decision had already been made, Saul had already been elected king by God, and all that was left was the formalities. Saul was carrying the title and the position of honor before lifting a finger.

Our Position in Heavenly Places

> *Then Samuel brought Saul and his servant into the hall and seated them at the head of those who were invited—about thirty in number.... So the cook took up the thigh with what was on it and set it in front of Saul. Samuel said, "Here is what has been kept for you. Eat, because it was set aside for you for this occasion from the time I said, 'I have invited guests.'" And Saul dined with Samuel that day.* (1 Samuel 9:22–24)

Saul is given the seat of high honor next to the prophet at the banquet table, and he is offered the choice meat. This is a picture of our position in the heavenly place next to our Savior Jesus Christ. We are elected and honored at a seat next to the King of Kings from the moment we meet Him, and we are given access to the best heaven can offer from the moment we enter His kingdom. Ephesians 2:6 says, *"God raised us up with Christ and seated us with him in the heavenly realms in Christ Jesus."*

This honor and blessing does not come after we have proven ourselves to be worthy, have served Him diligently for years, or have passed trials and tribulations. This honor was given to Saul before he was officially declared king of the tribes of Israel, and before he defeated the Philistines. In the same way, an honor worthy of a king is the inheritance we have in Christ. It is given to us only because of who He is and what He accomplished through His death and resurrection.

> *Then Samuel took a flask of olive oil and poured it on Saul's head and kissed him, saying, "Has not the* Lord *anointed you ruler over his inheritance?"* (1 Samuel 10:1)

A kingly anointing is not earned; it is given. God commanded Samuel to act, and Samuel obeyed and anointed Saul. The same principle is true for us believers. The moment we are saved, we are anointed as kings and queens, and we are given kingdom assignments. We are empowered by God to be rulers. How we feel about ourselves; the weakened state in which we enter into His kingdom; how ugly we feel inside or outside; what we have done or have not done in the past; all our past failures, character flaws, and bad habits—none of it really matters. Once we are saved, we are kings and queens with the full rights and privileges that come with it; we have to receive this identity by faith to operate in it.

We all come into the kingdom of God with some form of brokenness. That is why we needed a Savior. It is hard for broken men and women to see themselves as empowered kings and queens right after believing in Christ as Savior. But we receive all things in the kingdom through faith, and our identity is no different.

We are what we believe in our heart. Saul must have asked himself what was going on. How did he end up there, next to Samuel, and what made him so special that he could be the king of Israel? It is very important to note that although Saul may have felt inadequate in the selection, he did not object to or reject the calling and election of God.

Many times, God tries to promote and encourage us to see what He sees, but false humility takes hold of us. We want to act humble and meek and say things like, "No, I am not good enough to do that," "I am not worthy enough for such a calling," or "There are more qualified folks out there for the job." Well, that may be true—in fact, I am certain there are more qualified, smarter, and stronger people than me—but God chose us for our destiny.

We all were elected and chosen by God and crowned as kings and queens in His kingdom. We have to step into our destiny, accept our assignment, and allow Him to anoint and empower us to accomplish our kingdom task. We need to believe not only that we are qualified but that we are perfect for the job.

We all were elected and chosen by God and crowned as kings and queens in His kingdom. We have to step into our destiny, accept our assignment, and allow Him to anoint and empower us to accomplish our kingdom task.

When you look in the mirror, what do you see? When you speak, what do you hear? In my years in the ministry, I have heard God's people say things like, "I just can't do it! I am not able to go on anymore!" "I am not cut out for this type of ministry or warfare!" "I am too afraid to do this!" "I am not strong enough or anointed like so-and-so." The list goes on.

The fact is that we are and always will be able to do our kingly assignment. Although God is in the habit of picking out failures like me and you to come into His service, He has never asks failures like us to continue to fail while in His service. He is a master craftsman and designer. He takes great pleasure in taking broken vessels, and turning them into masterful works of art, worthy to be placed in the temple of God as an instrument of worship.

We all know that Saul did not finish his race well; his life ended in tragedy. But he started out doing the right things. He accepted his calling and believed in his destiny. This is very important because many of us never see ourselves as greater than our past failures. We need to see ourselves in the victories assigned to and laid before us by the Lord.

God Will Confirm Our Assignment

I need to share one last part of this story before closing this chapter. It answers that big question that people ask me: How will I know that a venture is my kingly assignment? I believe that God will send you confirmations of His leading just as He did with me with the Chinese opportunities, and as He did with Saul in our story.

Samuel had some detailed instructions for Saul. First, he let him know that the donkeys had been found, which relieved Saul of his earthly father's assignment. Then, Samuel gave Saul two prophetic words to confirm that God had chosen him to be appointed as the king of Israel.

The first word to Saul was that he would meet three men with two loaves of bread in their hands who were on their way to worship God. When they offered their bread to Saul, he was to accept it. As Saul traveled on, Samuel told him to go to a place of worship, Gibeah; there, he would meet a procession of prophets playing their harps and timbrels, praying and prophesying before the Lord. Samuel told Saul a remarkable thing that would happen next:

> *The Spirit of the Lord will come powerfully upon you, and you will prophesy with them; and you will be changed into a different person. Once these signs are fulfilled, do whatever your hand finds to do, for God is with you.* (1 Samuel 10:6–7)

All the things Samuel spoke to Saul were good news for him. They are good news for us as well. First, either our donkeys have been found or will be found soon. When people come to Jesus with their list of problems, or lost donkeys, all they care about is finding them. Well, the first thing God usually does is help them find them, since they were nothing more than a vehicle to lead you to Jesus. They are simply stepping-stones in finding your destiny.

Remember, when I got saved, I had a long list of problems and issues that seemed to be impossible to solve. They seemed like Mount Everest to me, and I had no earthly idea how to overcome them. The only way this stubborn Iranian Muslim kid was going to acknowledge Jesus as God's only Son was to lose a bunch of donkeys—and I mean a bunch. I had to get so desperate that I could not turn to anyone else except Him.

In the end, He solved my problems, and He miraculously delivered me from what I saw as my personal hell. Don't get caught up in immediate problems or challenges. Your lost donkeys will turn up, and you have God's Word and promise to hold on to.

After Samuel told Saul not to worry about his immediate concerns, he told him to go to Gibeah near the Philistine outpost. Gibeah was a hill belonging to God, but there was a problem—there was a Philistine outpost on it! There should not be a Philistine outpost on a hill belonging to God! So Samuel sent Saul to a place where he could recognize his kingly assignment. He was to go to a place that belonged to God but was now owned by the enemy. His assignment? To defeat the Philistines and retake the land. On the way to receive his assignment, Saul encountered prophets who spoke to him, and, for the first time in his life, Saul prophesied as well, confirming that his assignment was from God, and that he should never doubt his destiny.

This is incredible! Once you receive Christ, you not only receive the place and honor of a king, but you are promised your own Gibeah. Now, you may ask, what and where is Gibeah for you? How will you recognize it, and when will you know it?

For many of us, our past experiences, our brokenness, and what God calls us out of become our Gibeah. For a drug addict, it may be helping to free others from addiction; for a prostitute, it may be reaching out to save young girls from the vicious cycle of sexual abuse;

for a divorcee, it may be a deep desire to help those who are caught in the same cycle of depression and loss; for a businessman or businesswoman, it may be the revelation why he or she was given skills to succeed and a revelation of what to use his or her resources for; and, for a woman who has a child at a young age, it may be compassion to minister to a new generation of young unwed mothers. For a young Muslim kid from Iran, it was a calling to take the gospel to Muslims to free them from the same bondage he was delivered from. Although not everyone is called to take back territory from the place they were called out of, many of us are.

What is your kingdom assignment? What has been or is burning in your heart today? What are your dreams and which mountain do you wish to conquer for Him? What ideas keep you up at night? What destiny is calling your name? You need to know this mountain, and you need to visit it often until you have the courage and resources to conquer it.

Your Gibeah has to be big enough and important enough for you to pay the price of success. God calls us into ventures, and is willing to work miracles to assist us in getting there, but we still have to sow diligence, hard work, faith, patience, perseverance, and courage into the land of promise. Just like Joshua, we have to cross the Jordan and fight the giants to take what belongs to us.

Know what you are fighting for and recognize that your assignment is greater than you are, greater than any dream you can conjure up for yourself. It's worth the fight and it's worth the risk.

Do you believe you can do all things in Christ? Then charge up the hill of Gibeah, and kick the enemy out of what legally belongs to you! Press in to your calling, and believe that He who has called you into this good work is faithful to help you finish it with victory! (See 1 Thessalonians 5:24.)

19

UNICAT ENGAGES THE WORLD

For "whoever calls on the name of the LORD shall be saved."
How then will they call on Him in whom they have not believed?
And how shall they believe in Him whom they have not heard?
And how shall they hear without a preacher? And how shall they
preach unless they are sent?
—Romans 10:13–15 (NKJV)

Today, UNICAT is living its best story, providing the funds for a worldwide ministry to Muslims. By God's grace, we are answering the question, *"How shall they believe in Him whom they have not heard?"* by taking the message of the gospel of Jesus Christ to the lost. It is Jesus' salvation message that saves lives today for eternity.

As I mentioned earlier, I pastored for the Muslim community churches in Houston and Austin for more than thirteen years. Then, in 2001, when the ministry of satellite television opened up to Iran, I founded CCM Evangelical Ministries specifically to reach Muslims for Christ through television. This ministry couldn't be run without financial resources, and this is exactly what UNICAT and IRA Consulting have provided through the years.

During the last sixteen years, CCM Evangelical Ministries has partnered with other Christian ministries around the globe to bring the gospel message to Muslims worldwide. Iran Alive Ministries (IAM), led by Dr. Hormoz Shariat, the "Billy Graham of Iran," has been an incredible partner in this mission to preach and teach the gospel to an ever-growing population of young and disenfranchised Muslims who are yearning to learn more about Christ and the Christian way of life. I have seen firsthand thousands of Muslims embrace Jesus, and have witnessed the transformation of the nation of Iran before my very eyes.

Through our association with Iran Alive Ministries and Network 7, over the last sixteen years, we have been broadcast on television in Iran, and have been part of a movement that has led over seventy thousand souls to Christ! These numbers have been confirmed with names and addresses of people who have been saved. Even more exciting is knowing that the unconfirmed converts—people who have never contacted us or given us details of their conversion—are estimated to be four to ten times the number of who actually have given their names! That is a staggering 280,000 to 700,000 souls! No matter the actual number, UNICAT and the financial resources it provides enable me to participate in this "God" moment in history, where heaven intervenes and God changes a nation in one of the darkest spiritual regions in the world.

This is how the power of God works in our lives when we are willing to be used by Him. We may be small, but He is great and marvelous, and uses us to fulfill His purposes. I am so honored to have been and continue to be a part of what God is doing throughout the earth today to expand His love and His kingdom.

Right now, the underground church in Iran is expanding at a rapid rate. By population percentages, some have said that the fastest growing Christian church in the world is hidden in Iran! Some estimate that it is well over three million strong and growing daily. Of course, the growing church must be underground. No buildings, much secrecy. But countless Iranians are searching for real answers to the violence and emptiness that Islam brings to their personal lives.

Amazingly, it's predominantly young people who are responding without fear to the Gospel message. We are calling it "an awakening." These young people are seeking the kind of peace and unconditional love that only God the Father and His Son Jesus offer the world. On the IAM website, Dr. Hormoz Shariat reports, "Young people in Iran are now so open to Christ. The generation in their early twenties and younger often call or write to say, 'I was watching your satellite television program, and something in me said I need Jesus, and I'm ready.' No questions about Islam and Christianity. No fear of Islam or the government. Just, they are ready to choose Christ."[1] If the current trend continues, experts predict that the number of Christians in Iran will exceed seven million by 2020!

But the awakening is no longer limited to Iran; other nations in the region are also being touched. In spite of—undoubtedly, because of—the horrific persecution of Christians in Afghanistan, Iraq, and Syria, the church is growing within these people groups, and UNICAT is excited to be involved in this effort. By partnering with ministries that reach out to Syrian and Afghani refugees in Lebanon, Turkey, and

---

1. Hormoz Shariat, "5 Reasons Iran's Youth Are Ready to Choose Christ," (20 September 2016), https://hormozshariat.com/2016/09/20/5-reasons-irans-youth-are-ready-to-choose-christ.

Germany, we are serving as an instrument of love to a broken and hurting people who have lost everything. Whether supplying food, clothing, or medication, UNICAT and IRA Consulting provide assistance to ease the suffering of those afflicted by constant war and conflict in the region. This is the greatest move of God since the early Christian church, and we are a part of it. I am eternally grateful to the Lord for placing me in the middle of His work among these people. I am walking in the fullness of my destiny.

I would like to share a few stories of the amazing things that are happening with Iranians all across the globe. I have witnessed some of these stories; others have been shared with my team and our partners over the years. I have to say that there have been so many testimonies that volumes of books could be written about them. Here, I will share just a few of those testimonies.

Testimony One: God's Power in Iran

"My name is Afrouz, and I am a twenty-four-year-old woman living in Iran. For most of my teenage years, I battled anxiety and depression. My family had financial problems, which created tension and disagreements in all of our relationships. Many nights, as I cried myself to sleep, I felt the best thing for me would simply be to die. I was thankful to finally find my first job at the age of twenty-one, but then misfortune hit again.

"I had been experiencing a lot of fatigue and weakness that are uncommon for a young woman my age. I made several trips to the doctors, always hoping to hear good news that whatever I was going through would be only temporary. Then came the diagnosis; I had multiple sclerosis. My decline happened quickly; it seemed as though every part of my body was failing before my eyes. The Iranian doctors were no longer able to help me. I became sicker with each passing day, and I wondered, *Is there any hope for life's pain?*

"I don't want my testimony to seem as though it has no powerful ending, because it does. However, in the midst of my physical suffering, my father passed away. Financially, this should have meant the end for my mother and our family. Even though the company I had formerly worked for was still helping us and taking care of my medical needs, we were in a terrible position. At the time, I was partially paralyzed, unable to take care of myself. I had little hope and was lost in the darkness.

"Then into this darkness stepped a ray of hope. My uncle had left the Muslim faith and become a Christian believer. On one of his visits, he brought me a Bible written in the Farsi language and told me that if I believed in Jesus Christ, He would heal me. I started to read the Bible from that very day and I liked it, even though I could not understand what much of it meant for me.

"One day, even though I was barely able to flip the channels on the television, I came across your broadcast. The minister spoke of the power and love of God, which changes us from the inside out, and how the Bible will give us the guidelines for life in the kingdom of God—the Christian God I knew so little about. After that, I regularly watched your television programs. Soon, with the guidance of God's Holy Spirit, I was able to understand what I was reading in the Bible, including the power of God for salvation in Jesus Christ.

"I was still able to move very little, so I asked my mother to help me call your program, and I prayed with the staff. I was crying hard, repenting of all my sins; as I was praying, I noticed that I could move my hands and legs! I was filled with such joy, such happiness! I cannot possibly describe what I felt as my mother helped me to get out of my bed. Jesus healed me that day, and now I am a healthy young lady. I can never thank God enough for loving me and saving me inside and out!

"A short time later, two beautiful Christians came from your ministry to visit me; it was like having a visit from angels! They are now spending time with me, teaching me how to study the Word of God and how to live a life that brings Him glory. I can't tell you how grateful I am for your ministry and for everything you do for Iranians. I pray for you and your ministry daily."

Testimony Two: From the Mouth of Babes

"My name is Mehran. I am ten years old and live in Tehran with my family. My parents are helping me to explain the miracle that happened to me. Until five weeks ago, I was paralyzed from neck to toe, but now I am healed! This is how the miracle happened: A friend of my dad told us that Jesus Christ is a healer and, if we prayed in His name, I would receive His healing. He also told us to read the Bible and to watch your satellite television programs so that we could get to know all about Jesus, God's Son.

"We had nothing to lose, so we started watching your television programs. We were glad to hear of the love that God had for people and how He wanted to bring them salvation in Jesus Christ.

"One day, with the help of my dad, I called your program and talked to one of your counselors. After praying with her to receive Jesus as my Savior, she asked me, 'Do you believe that Jesus hears your prayers and wants to heal you? Do you believe that nothing is impossible for Him and you can receive His healing?'

"I answered yes, and she prayed for me. Ten minutes after hanging up with that counselor, I started to feel warmth in my whole body, and our house was filled with the sweet smell of vanilla. I knew in my heart that the Holy Spirit I had heard about from your teachings was right there with me. I believed that God wanted to give me whatever I asked for in that moment. So, with all my heart, I asked Him to heal me.

"God's peace filled my house! I was completely overwhelmed with the presence of God, and I just knew I was healed. As my parents stood beside me, I got up and started to walk. I was praising the Lord! For the first time in my life, I was able to climb the stairs to the second floor of our house using my own legs!

"I am calling you to testify to the miracle that Jesus brought into my life and also to thank you for your television programs, your ministry, and your counselors. Jesus has healed me physically and healed my whole family spiritually. My family and friends know that only a miracle could have let me walk again, and I tell them that Jesus is the one who did this miracle for me!"

Testimony Three: Raising Up the Wrong Man

This unusual testimony comes from a couple in our ministry who serve in Iran:

"We were just informed that the father of one of our house church members had become gravely ill and was taken to the hospital. We rushed there to comfort our friends, but once we got there, we could not locate them. So I asked which room in the intensive care unit they were keeping the father. We hoped to find the family and pray with them.

"Once we reached the intensive care unit, we inquired about the man's health, and the nurse quietly said, 'I am sorry to inform you, sir, but the patient you are inquiring about has just passed away, and he is being prepared to be sent to the hospital morgue.'

"We stood there shocked, as this had happened so quickly. I asked the nurse if my wife and I could go to his room to pay our last respects, and she said okay but to do it quickly as this was not normal hospital policy.

"As we entered the room, we saw a man completely covered with a white sheet. We were sure we were in the right room, so we just looked at each other and said, 'So what do we do?'

"My wife answered, 'We don't have to accept this. We have the power of God to raise the dead. Jesus did it with Lazarus, and Paul did it, too—so can we.'

"Well, I agreed, but I wasn't sure if this crazy idea was going to work. We both prayed and asked God to bring our friend's father back to life as a gift to all of us.

"After our prayer, it seemed that nothing had changed. So we left the room and went downstairs with the hope of finding our friends and intending to comfort them as best we could. As we reached the next floor, there they were in the waiting lounge. Something very strange was going on—none of them were crying or seemed overtly distraught.

"I thought to myself, *Well, they are taking the news pretty well.* We approached them and said hello, and before I could give my condolences, our friend said, 'Brother, there has been a miracle. When they brought our father in today, he was so ill that we were worried about his very life. But we started praying, and the good news is that we have a good report that he is recovering well. He is out of danger.'

"As I listened to him, I was thinking, *Who was the man my wife and I prayed for upstairs?* Sitting there confused and yet happy for my friend, I noticed a family crying and grieving in the same waiting lounge. I felt sure that this was the family related to the man we had prayed for upstairs in the hospital room. At that very moment, a nurse hurriedly came in and started calling the other family by name. She was so very excited and animated. She was talking about a miracle and that their father was not dead! He was up and awake asking for them!

"My wife and I looked at each other and were filled with sheer joy; we had to see this for ourselves. We had to let this family know that it was Jesus who did this miracle for them. We excused ourselves and followed the now jubilant family upstairs.

"Yes, it was the same exact room that we had gone to earlier to pray. To say that there was a commotion in that room would be a great understatement! But how would we prove that Jesus did the miracle and not sound like we were crazy? After all, there was no one there who actually saw us praying for the corpse in the room.

"Just about that time, we heard the old man from inside the room asking his family, 'Where is the couple that came and prayed for me? I need to see them and thank them.'

"He continued asking them loudly to help him find us, and we could not hold back anymore. We walked joyfully into the room and, before we could even say a word, the old man started shouting, 'It was you! It was you! Thank you for saving me from death! I saw you both praying for me when I was lying in the room. As soon as you left, I felt I was pushed back into my body. How can I thank you and thank Jesus, the One in whose name you prayed?'

"Well, as you can imagine, we got to share the good news with all of them, and the man and his entire family received salvation in Christ that day. What a wonderful case of mistaken identity! By the way, our friend's father was released the following day from the hospital."

Reaching the World for Jesus

Today through CCM Evangelical Ministries, my team and I have several hands of ministry reaching out to Muslims around the world. Our online church has 1,500 to 2,000 weekly attendees, and our online telegram portal has more than 2,500 attendees, who download the program and share it with their families and friends, often in secret house meetings. This means that thousands more hear these messages each week. During the past sixteen years, we have encouraged and trained hundreds and hundreds of Iranian pastors, and now we have expanded our training to pastors and leaders from Egypt, Syria, Lebanon, Iraq, Tajikistan, Afghanistan, and Georgia, to name a few. We bring them out of the country for safety reasons, train them, and then send them back to lead others to Christ.

We have an online Bible college called New Life College, which currently has four hundred thirty former Muslim students enrolled. Our weekly television programs are still recorded in Houston and broadcast via satellite all over Asia and the Middle East. More than three hundred thousand people in Iran watch these programs each week. Four hundred thousand to five hundred thousand in the predominately Muslim countries of eastern Asia watch our weekly programs on ISAAC Television.

My latest mission was leading a CCM Evangelical Ministries team on a two-week trip to Egypt, Lebanon, and Germany to encourage Iranian and Arab Christian pastors. First, we flew to Egypt to sponsor a conference for fifty Christian pastors. We paid for all their expenses—transportation, lodging, and food—so they could attend. I believe we are called to encourage and empower these men of God who are bringing the gospel to Muslims in Egypt, Iran, and beyond. Through UNICAT, we have the resources to help them build their ministry for the kingdom.

Next, we traveled to Lebanon, where our mission looked quite different. We visited dozens of refugee camps, supplying as many people as possible with food, clothing, and shoes. I am beyond blessed that, through our business resources, we can bring them the necessities they desperately need, and can also share the love and salvation of Christ as the opportunities present themselves.

As people are well-aware today, millions of Muslims live in Europe, and our vision to reach Muslims with the gospel extends there as well. We encourage, teach, and support a network of Iranian pastors through our broadcasts, and our giving to England, France, Norway, and Denmark. So at the end this mission trip, we spent five days in Germany, leading a conference of Iranian pastors and leaders who are enrolled in our online Bible college. These leaders joined us from several countries in Europe to hear the Word of God, and to be encouraged and strengthened in their work in Muslim communities. CCM Evangelical Ministries was able to provide everything needed for the conference—lodging, food, and speakers. Using God's resources from UNICAT simply confirms in my heart that the company truly belongs to Him.

On an upcoming mission trip, I will travel to Tajikistan, Georgia, Turkey, Lebanon, Egypt, and Sweden to work with pastors and leaders who are at the front lines for Christ.

CCM Evangelical Ministries is very active in Georgia, located south of Russia on the shore of the Black Sea. There are many Persian-speaking people in the nation, and we have teamed with a network of ministries at work there. Recently, we helped to build a home where people can stay to overcome addictions. Roadside food stands have been set up in many areas of the nation to minister to truck drivers. We share our food and God's way of salvation through Jesus Christ with them. The Christian leader who is spearheading this work is also supported by our ministry.

Just like the rest of the body of Christ, we are painfully aware of the refugee crisis in Turkey. During the past several years, CCM Evangelical Ministries has financially supported multiple churches in Turkey that have reached out to hundreds of refugees with food, clothing, and hope.

Not all our support goes directly to Bible ministries. The world is full of people in desperate need of compassion. CCM Evangelical Ministries has a humanitarian fund that has been used to dig a number of wells in Liberia, where people are desperate for a clean water supply. Do we share the gospel with them? Of course we do; it is their saving grace for all eternity. But they receive the blessing of a clean water supply regardless of their response to the gospel message. I thank God every day for income from UNICAT, His company, which touches so many people around the world.

This is not now and never has been about me and accumulating great wealth. It is about God speaking a word, and then bringing it to pass for His glory. The dream that has been closest to my heart for all these years is now flourishing around the world.

The biggest blessing is that I do not have to raise money to do the work God has called me to do. UNICAT pays for it all. That was the vision given to the woman who spoke that prophetic word to me almost twenty-seven years ago, that money would fall out of my pockets, and would bless the church. This is not now and never has been about me and accumulating great wealth. It is about God speaking a word, and then bringing it to pass for His glory. The dream that has been closest to my heart for all these years is now flourishing around the world.

We Are a People of Purpose

Every Christian is called to some purpose, and an incredible destiny awaits all who seek the Lord. Those who are called to the field of commerce are called not only for themselves, but for what they can accomplish in the transfer of wealth into the kingdom of God. Obviously, people have achieved success, and will continue to do so without God and without special heavenly help. But for Christians, success without God and receiving glory for it is no success at all.

Every Christian is called to some purpose, and an incredible destiny awaits all who seek the Lord. Those who are called to the field of commerce are called not only for themselves, but for what they can accomplish in the transfer of wealth into the kingdom of God.

I believe that we Christians carry a greater sense of responsibility than others to take our ideas and concepts more seriously, and pursue business plans that keep popping up in our heads. Consider that these ideas may not be just a fluke, but God's gentle nudge to help us move forward in our life journey toward success. After all, we are doing it for all the people who will be touched directly and indirectly by our business ventures.

We are a people of purpose driven by this innate and internal flame that burns inside us the moment we come to know Jesus and His great love. We know that such an incredible grace should not be wasted or thrown away on a life that accomplishes little or, worse, nothing of value at all. We know that God would not do as much as He has done for us if He did not have a deeper mission and greater journey awaiting us if we trust in Him.

So my hope is that now, after reading my story, you are energized, excited, uplifted, and empowered with a new sense of purpose. I pray that you are filled with hope that if God could use a seventeen-year-old Iranian immigrant who came to the United States by himself to do all that has been done up to this point, He can and will use you and your life to do great and mighty things in the world today.

May this story encourage God's people to pursue their dreams and godly destinies and endure until victory is experienced! I pray that my story will be repeated thousands of times in the lives of others, and that God's kings, queens, and priests will be activated to go and take the mountain He has predestined for them to occupy for His name's sake.

Let God take you to the other side of the Jordan, and plant you in your own promised land, a land of milk and honey, a land of success, and the abundance of provision. Be assured, you are absolutely called to success. You are a decision away from starting your life journey in Him. I encourage you to step into your destiny, walk the walk of faith, overcome your fears, and trust in the One who is the God of the impossible!

> *Now to Him who is able to do exceedingly abundantly above all that we ask or think, according to the power that works in us, to Him be glory in the church by Christ Jesus to all generations, forever and ever. Amen.* (Ephesians 3:20–21 NKJV)

ABOUT THE AUTHOR

Mani Erfan was born and raised in Iran as a Shiite Muslim. He experienced the fall of the Shah and the coming of the Islamic revolution to the country first-hand in 1979. After the start of the Iran-Iraq war in 1980, Mani immigrated to United States alone at the young age of sixteen in 1983 to pursue his studies. Mani finished his degree in Chemical Engineering from University of Florida with high honors in 1988 and moved to Houston, Texas, to pursue his professional career.

After a miraculous encounter with Jesus Christ while attending college, he converted to Christianity in 1987. Mani has been working in the professional field of catalysis since 1989 and was one of the founders of UNICAT Catalyst Technologies in 1999, a multi-million-dollar global catalyst sales and service company.

Today, UNICAT has offices worldwide with sales exceeding five hundred million dollars since its inception. Since 1993, Mani has also been involved in Christian ministry and missions, first as a local pastor and then as the founder and CEO of CCM Evangelical Ministries, which uses media and satellite TV to bring the gospel of Jesus Christ to millions of Muslims worldwide. CCM's ministry is extremely active in the Middle East and Central Asia, and includes local missions and outreaches in many diverse Muslim nations.

To find out more, go to manierfan.com.